THE ART OF
Gardening in Pots

THE ART OF
Gardening in Pots

Elisabeth de Lestrieux

Hazel Evans

PHOTOGRAPHS
Kees Hageman, Rudolf Bom and Anton Schlepers

ANTIQUE COLLECTORS' CLUB

© Original edition *(Pot Sierlijk)* 1988 Lannoo, Tielt and Terra Zutphen
© English edition 1990 Antique Collectors' Club Ltd.; reprinted 1996

ISBN 1 85149 131 7

British Library Cataloguing-in-Publication Data
A catalogue record for this book is available from the British Library

Designed by Geert Verstaen
Printed in Belgium by Lannoo, Tielt

CONTENTS

NTRODUCTION

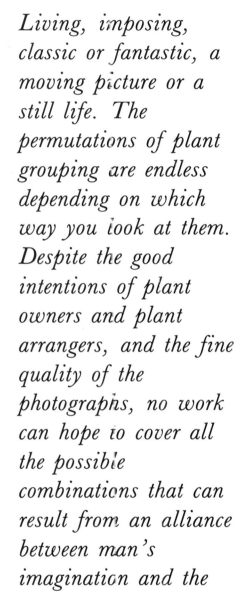

Living, imposing, classic or fantastic, a moving picture or a still life. The permutations of plant grouping are endless depending on which way you look at them. Despite the good intentions of plant owners and plant arrangers, and the fine quality of the photographs, no work can hope to cover all the possible combinations that can result from an alliance between man's imagination and the

hand of nature. All this book can do, then, at the very least, is to introduce plant lovers to this fascinating world which beckons, in the hope that it will encourage them to explore it further themselves.

We will be showing you some new plant varieties, including some that are not very well known, taking care to give them botanical names that are as correct as possible. With this in mind, the text has been carefully checked by experts and we are most grateful to them for their help.

We would also like to thank the many horticultural suppliers, as well as the potters and importers of terracotta for the containers, ranging from the very simple to the most sophisticated, which served as a showcase for the plant arrangements.

This book would not have been possible without the enthusiasm of three specialist plant photographers. Kees Hageman captured some beautiful species and varieties as well as the splendours of his roof terrace and those of famous gardens. Living near me as he does, Rudolf Bom never ceased to

respond to my appeals to photograph this or that plant in full flower. And I must not forget the contribution of Anton Schlepers for the photographs of plants and flowers in his own garden.

On the opposite page, the vivid blooms of *Datura sanguinea* (sometimes known as *Brugmansia sanguinea*) dominate the plant, though they do not, unfortunately, contribute any scent. It is easy to get over this, however, by placing it alongside strongly perfumed plants. That is why we have put it with the scented-leaved geranium *Pelargonium odoratissimum,* the prince of perfumers adorned with a velvety cloak. In spring a fresh lemon scent wafts from the modest *Polygala chamaebuxus* in their little pots. In summer the task is taken over by the trailing *Jasminum polyanthum.* And if *Angelica archangelica* orchestrates this symphony of scents, the subtle orange nuances of *Idesia polycarpa* bring a final touch to the delicate colour range of the group.

In the course of our work, colours and scents, plain and decorative shapes, luxury and simplicity, gardens and terraces never ceased to be a source of inspiration. We hope that this book of pictures interlaced with text will give readers some of the pleasure we had in producing it. In any case, we wish them the best of luck in working with containers and their contents, and plenty of imagination to stamp their own personality on their gardens. Above all, we hope they have the time and tranquillity that is needed to translate their own talent and ideas into flower pictures.

Elisabeth de Lestrieux

CLIPPED SHAPES

Box, with its minute shiny green leaves, is an amenable plant which can be very easily clipped into many different forms and shapes. It is also a particularly good subject for growing in pots. Box can be used in many ways, but it looks at its most elegant when it is presented in pairs — globes, pyramids and spirals adorning gardens, sited on the curves of pathways and shown off in niches.

Planted in a square at the cross-roads of two little paths (top), four pyramids of clipped box jut out of a dense carpet of emerald green ivy. They mount guard close to a picket garden gate to the right of the picture, whose white wooden slats make a perfect contrast to the surrounding greenery. In the same garden (above) two shaggy spheres of box emphasise the privacy of an old fern-patterned garden seat

romantically nestling under a rose arch. On the opposite page, two clipped spirals of box point their tips towards a rose arch and an acacia.

Pot-grown box (*Buxus*) will resist hard winters without difficulty. In the case of really hard frosts, however, or if the day and night temperatures plunge to -10 degrees celsius (14 degrees fahrenheit) for several consecutive weeks, it is wise

to transfer them to a cool frost-free spot or a cold greenhouse. When climatic conditions improve, the box should be placed out of doors again, to prevent it from putting on new growth too early.

If the pots are too heavy to be moved, however, they can be wrapped in straw and put in plastic sacks to protect the roots from frost damage.

The two preceding pages show a host of stylish shapes in elegant containers, all painstakingly maintained. They illustrate the gardens of a horticultural company known throughout Europe for the quality and imagination of its collection which is particularly prized by many garden lovers – Giardini of Kalmthout, where you can buy some wonderful things. Giardini is the showcase of a company that specialises in ornaments for terraces, orangeries, gardens and in topiary too – clipped shrubs in diverse and interesting pots. Standard bay trees, for instance, with twisted trunks show off their baroque curves. From the time a young sapling unfurls its first leaves, it takes dozens of years to

obtain a perfect specimen with a good mop head like these. The photograph on pages 40 and 41 show two examples that I have on my own terrace. Although they are certainly simpler than those on the preceding pages, the latter, nevertheless, are at least twenty-five years old. Naturally much of Giardini's topiary consists of items in *Buxus sempervirens,* but they also use juniper and cypress cut into balls, tiers or columns, capped by domes grafted on to other species. Most of the terracotta containers come from Italy, but the pale pots are from the kilns at Biot, in the Midi of France. The elegant putti are figures symbolising two of the four seasons, and date from 1880.

Two tall spirals of box surrounded by a profusion of different plants, are the key elements of the plant composition on the opposite page, enhanced, at the far end, under the window of the house, by a curious bench which is built in the shape of a wheelbarrow. The colours of the house itself and the courtyard blend well with the different greens of the plants. On the left of the courtyard, the containers huddle under the shelter of large leaves of a *Magnolia grandiflora*. In northern regions this superb plant is, alas, often only for those who are able to take it into a conservatory to protect it from hard frosts. You can see a beautiful example in the conservatory on pages 24 and 25. Close cropped box prefers to be in large containers where its roots can develop and grow with ease. However, you can use a smaller pot if you fertilise the soil regularly. But it is wise to take certain precautions. Ornamenting the surface of the soil with heavy stones or placing other plants in the same soil are two things to avoid: they upset the balance and drain the soil of its natural resources. The only exceptions to this rule are prostrate thyme and creeping mint (*Mentha requienii*) which will carpet the surface and scent the air but tend to make it difficult to apply fertiliser.

A pathway (left), is bordered with standard *Catalpa bignonioides* 'Aurea' standing in square containers. Their sharp yellow-green complements the darker colour of the line of clipped box beneath to great effect.

Tennis courts are hidden away between high hornbeam hedges (*Carpinus betulus*) leading up to a statue (below). The deep green shiny leaves of the rounded and conical box topiary in its line of pots punctuates the imposing screen at intervals, accentuating the tranquillity of the pathway.

Easy to trim and sculpt, a variety of small-leaved privet finds a permanent home on my own terrace (right). But my Chinese privet (*Ligustrum delavayanum* or *L. ionandrum*) is, unfortunately, not very resistant to cold. Nevertheless, I have had the peacock on a stem for more than four years. The simple fact of transferring it to a cool but frost-free place during periods of sharp frost and taking it out immediately afterwards to allow it to grow normally appears to be enough to assure its survival. Both the peacock and the bird (also carefully shaped by me) produce a profusion of flowers, transforming them in season into animals with white fur. If they then tend to lose their sharp outlines, it is easy to restore the shape by clipping them immediately after flowering.

Destined to set off the top of a hedge with which they will eventually blend, animal figures (such as swans or chickens) mounted on trellis make interesting topiary subjects. These figures develop very quickly trained on a frame and ivy can be used to cover the gaps while it is growing.

Anyone who wants to clip an almost instant pyramid shape can do so within a year by cultivating *Kochia scoparia* (var. *trichophylla*) whose clear green foliage is visible in the left background opposite. There is also another form – variegated with white, *Kochia* 'Acapulco Silver', which is transformed into a symphony of purple in autumn.

On the table opposite is ample proof of how well hostas grow in pots. This example is *Hosta undulata* 'Vitata'; five vigorous little plants have entirely covered the surface of the pot in less than two years. The front of the picture is highlighted by an extraordinary ornament of three terracotta cushions bordered with braid which comes from Italy. To its right the entire group bathes in the summer fragrance of a lovely gardenia.

Of Poodles and mushrooms

On the left two magnificent 'poodles', as I call them, guard the superb terraces of the Chateau de 's Gravenwezel, in the province of Antwerp, the luxurious background for the celebrated collection of May and Axel Vervoort, antique dealers.

The 'poodle' cut for plants has been known since the beginning of time, and is done in a similar way to the clip given to poodles. Ancient engravings show shrubs consisting of two or three tiers, if not more, cut in this fashion. The three-tiered 'poodles' in question are cut in Chinese privet (*Ligustrum lucidum*), a plant which produces clusters of white blooms in the course of flowering. An example of one in flower can be seen in the conservatory on page 26. Today you can easily obtain many cultivated forms of these shrubs. You need to treat them like *Ligustrum delavayanum* mentioned on page 14. The two topiary mushrooms framing a stylish house (below) were clipped by their owner in myrtle (*Myrtus communis* 'Compacta') and are five years old. This variety grows vigorously and keeps a good dense yet compact silhouette.

These pages show a garden which features herbs and flowers to cut for the house in the lovely estate of the Chateau de s'Gravenwezel. Two pools of still water in the centre of a main pathway lie either side of an 18th century blue stone sundial which stands on a velvet cruciform tapestry of scented mint.

This area is surrounded by plants arranged in colours and planted in shapes corresponding to motifs in the apartments and annexes of the chateau.

The elements that make up this plant palette play second fiddle to the colours of the flowers. Thus the new orangery, from which this picture was taken (see page 31), is flanked with hellebores with blooms of a mainly green colouring, their pendulous clusters of flowers followed by beak-like seed pods. In addition there is every possible variety of euphorbia, that can stand winter cold, as well as artemisias, whose silver foliage and tiny balls of green flowers go so well in bouquets. Then comes the emerald of the China rose (*Rosa chinensis* 'Viridiflora') which completes the plant mosaic.

The green coloured plants for cutting flower alongside herbs of the same tones, among them angelica (*A. archangelica*) and marjoram (*Origanum majorana*). These plants are sited according to height – the creeping mint comes first, the tallest plants being put in the furthest corners.

Along the borders, green and yellow give way to blue flowers planted in a horseshoe shape at the far end of the herb garden. And the eye is immediately drawn to two squares of catmint (*Nepeta* x *faassenii*). The arrangement of centre borders is a masterpiece, containing, successively, groups of blue roses (two lightly perfumed cultivars, 'Nil Bleu' and 'Blue Moon'), groups of late flowering *Hibiscus syriacus* 'Blue Bird', and the tall plumes of *Perovskia atriplicifolia* 'Blue Spire'.

After the blue garden comes the white garden, which flanks a large service path, its meandering curves encouraging you to follow its entire length and discover the flowers which are blooming along it. It leads to a rose garden where the parterres are covered by a silver mat of the non-flowering *Stachys byzantina* 'Silver Carpet'.

Leaving this far corner, the flowers for cutting change progressively from pale pink to bright pink, then to velvety red before giving way to yellow, apricot and a pale orange. We have now returned to the area of yellow flowers. Bamboos and an outcrop of grasses in one corner are of particular interest to lovers of the Orient, while a garden with contrasting leaves flanks the orangery. This garden has a splendid collection of plants with attractive leaves which are used in the making of bouquets.

Finally the only clipped shape in this well-arranged ensemble is a large standard clipped bay (*Lauris nobilis*).

CLIMBING SHAPES

Perennial climbers can make charming decorative pictures, and their good looks are well known. But you need to put them in a pot if you want to make the most of their seductive twining growth which, unfortunately, is very often incapable of resisting the rigours of winter.

Spirals and pyramids are two the most spectacular ways of showing climbers in pots. The picture (right) shows an example of the first – the coils of ivy with yellow-splashed leaves is *Hedera helix* 'Gold Heart'. On page 40 you can see two examples of passion flower (*Passiflora caerulea*) trailing elegantly over a frame and around terracotta pots. It is only half hardy in northern Europe and other temperate climes but, once sown, grows with great speed. Iron arches and frames, often reproductions of old styles, are particularly good for climbers and also for growing standard gooseberries which can be cultivated very well in pots.

On the left two arcs of the rose 'Peace' are trained over a classical wrought-iron shape.

Photographed in a hot climate an
arch of morning glory (*Ipomoea
learii*) is covered with intense violet
blooms which flower from June to
September. In such conditions this
climber can easily cover up to 10
metres (33ft.). A similar effect in
a colder climate could be achieved
with *Clematis durandii* which is frost
hardy, or *C. montana* which makes
a great deal of rapid growth and
flowers in early summer.

These and the following pages take us into the winter world of conservatories which are attached to houses. Capturing as they do every ray of sunshine, and efficiently protecting tender plants, these sanctuaries are havens of peace and beauty for their owners.

Layout is the most important factor in a conservatory. One of them illustrated here belongs to a doctor who uses it as a through way between his consulting rooms and his home, and the glassed passageway allows him to go from one building to the other and remain warm and dry.

On the extreme right, a glass awning marks the entry to the long passage through the conservatory.

Cascading delights

Conservatories make splendid shelter, particularly for edible climbing plants which normally only grow in hot climates.

The grape vine, for instance, would be an ideal candidate if it did not already exist in many forms adapted to northern climates. But, then, the grapes are only harvested after months of attentive care, just at the time our markets are full of cheap grapes cultivated in Greece, Italy or France, making it less advantageous to grow them ourselves. Better to be more adventurous and grow something more exotic.

Apart from its blue blooms and green leaves, it is possible to obtain countless combinations of colours with the edible fruits of the passion flower.

The deep purple fruits of *Passiflora edulis*, for instance, follow greenish-white flowers. The fruits are edible despite the fact that their skin is wrinkled, and their sugary flavour is most enjoyable. The fruits of *P. edulis* var. *flavicarpa* are yellow in colour and less wrinkled, but the fruit has a more insipid taste. The elegant oval fruit of *P. mollisima* has given it the nickname 'passion banana', while the perfumed white-fleshed oval fruits of

P. ligularis turn to an orange brown in time. *P. incarnata* is, perhaps, the most attractive of them all as its large flowers of 7-8 cm (2¾-3ins.) in diameter make a charming sight in purple and lavender tints, and its clear yellow fruits, like chicken's eggs, are particularly succulent.

The elegant range of giant leaves – as much as 20cm (8ins.) across – of the grape-like *Coccoloba uvifera* part in spring to show clusters of little perfumed flowers

which turn into edible 'grapes' which can be harvested at the end of the summer.

Billardiera longiflora is a species of climber with long-lasting leaves which change slowly from yellow-green to purple. After flowering in July, the clear blue oval berries, about 3cm (1¼ins.) long, appear in October. *B. longiflora* 'Fructo-albo' is a variety with white fruits.

Holboellia latifolia and *H. coriacea* are two other twining creepers with edible fruits which are particularly good to grow in a winter garden. Male and female appear on the same plant, but the pollinator – a tropical insect – is not, unfortunately, found in temperate climes, so man has to take over the work of nature by transferring the pollen with the aid of a little piece of cotton wool or a sable paintbrush. But the reward for this task soon appears in the form of little sausage-shaped purple fruits about 6-8cm (2½-3ins.) long. The greeny-white male flowers of *H. coriacea* appear on wood made the previous year. In contrast, the female flowers open on wood formed a year later.

Did you know that the faithful *Akebia* can also produce purple sausage-shaped fruits if the temperature is raised a little? Clusters of perfumed pink female flowers and smaller purple male blooms appear in April, though this early flowering makes chance pollination by insects more or less impossible. On the other hand, if *Akebia* is grown in the shelter of a conservatory, it is possible to hand pollinate the fruits with a small brush. A little tepid water sprinkled over the plants beforehand makes the transfer of the pollen from the stamens to the pistils easier. *Akebia trifoliata* produces sausage-shaped fruits 12cm (4¾ins.) long. In the case of *A. quinata,* the fruits are in the form of an egg about 6-8cm (2½-3ins.) long. In Japan these fruits are more appreciated for their jet black seeds than for their flavour which is relatively insipid. The skins can be grilled and served as an aperitif.

The charm of terraces

All around this converted farmhouse, whose gardens I designed, are long rectangular-shaped terraces linked by passages and flanked by recesses designed as little outdoor 'salons' with comfortable seats.

A large elegant conservatory has been installed on one of these terraces where, as well as sheltering from the rain, the family can enjoy the country view in autumn and winter.

On the preceding pages a large entrance porch opens on to a corridor of the main house. Sited on the corner is a fine *Magnolia grandiflora.* A fig, *Ficus carica,* has made itself comfortable here by the side of the garden door. Meanwhile, against the walls, espaliers support and guide camellias and roses.

It wasn't until the last century that conservatories began to be made entirely of glass. Until that time, although orangeries had large windows they didn't have glass roofs. The old-fashioned charm of this style of building which we show here is in the warm shelter of the walls of the Chateau de s'Gravenwezel, not far from Antwerp, which dates in part from the 12th century. The grounds contain some of the most well-known modern gardens.

As you can see, this orangery is not used exclusively for plants. All the same it gives shelter in winter to the citrus trees shown on pages 51, 52 and 53. It also makes a perfect background for a harmonious partnership of plants in pots and simple furniture. The long red pine table does not detract from the scene at all. Long since damaged by water, it integrates perfectly in the world of containers – old, new and reproduction – sheltering different species of plants. The best way to look at this indoor universe and take in the scents and the greenery is comfortably seated in a chair or sofa. Dating from the 19th century, the little terracotta trough, the bulbous one beside it (behind the chair) and the glazed pot that once held salt, all contain tropical and subtropical floating plants. The water lettuces (below), which are cultivated for their bizarre flowers, cannot stand the rigours of winter in northern European and other cold climates. Difficult to keep, they are, nevertheless, offered for sale each year in troughs by florists and garden centres. They multiply rapidly during spring and summer.

In these illustrations, we are still in the orangery featured on the previous pages. On the left, a 19th century dresser in red pine, originally from England, is literally covered with pots and vegetation. To its left, standing squarely on the floor, is a terracotta garden urn made around 1800 which contains a spindly, rather fragile looking lemon tree. On the dresser is a stone urn, also from England, while on the shelves are a number of old flower pots which have belonged to the chateau for generations. Other containers from the 19th century mount guard, while two tree stumps cast in concrete, to the right of the picture, are typical of a 1900s' fashion.

On the right hand page, a window of the orangery overlooks the garden of aromatic plants and flowers for cutting. On its sill an old pot, made at the end of the 17th or early 18th century, houses a *Stephanotis floribunda* whose stems have launched an assault round the window frame. Note the little ventilation gate ajar in the middle of the window.

The orangery of the Chateau de 's Gravenwezel is now integrated with a new complex constructed nearby. On the floor the original system of heating via wooden slats has been replaced by convected heat. On the next two pages the two rather arrogant looking busts in the shadows are the work of the neoclassical sculptor Gilles Lambert Godecharle who carved them in 1770.

The table on the left and the seats of Verona marble, decorated with lions' heads carved in the Roman manner, date from the 19th century. On the antique column near the window, an 18th century blue stone vase houses an exuberant sun-loving *Plectranthus*. Opposite, a *Sparmannia africana* benefits from the light given out through the high window.

POTS AND POTTERIES

This chapter gives you a chance to do a little lazy armchair shopping – for the garden, naturally. It takes you among the world of pots, urns, vases, bowls and other ornaments and gives you an opportunity to decide what you'll buy before going to a garden centre or supplier. On the following pages you will find a veritable treasure trove of modern shapes, as well as shapes inspired by antique designs. Genuine antique items are the subject of a separate chapter.

This display of decorative objects for the garden, with elegant antique pieces placed side by side with contemporary ones, comes from the collection of the horticultural establishment, Giardini, whom I have mentioned earlier.

The group of beautiful cast-iron vases on the left date from the 19th century. Some are painted, others simply varnished. The two metal birds were originally the trade signs of a poultry seller.

The two marble vases at the back of the table have to be kept inside to protect their finish. The two little bowls in pale faience, the pots and bowl-shaped vases, are from the ateliers of Biot, near Grasse in the Alpes Maritimes. On the right of this group are two old jugs which served as containers for calvados or oil – who knows? – similar to those believed to be of Berber origin. Under the bust is an Italian cornucopia of fruits with a man-made patina, out of which cascade pomegranates, grapes and pineapples. To the right of this are two French vases dating from the 19th century. To the extreme right, placed on the floor, is a large French grain container.

When one buys pottery or hand-made vases, whether or not they are antique, it is important to know whether it is possible to leave them out of doors during winter in a cold climate. If you are not sure, then it is wiser to use them for half hardy plants that you will remember to bring in during periods of frost.

This impressive collection of terracotta objects shows just a sample of the diversity of forms and decorations that are available from different parts of Europe. The containers in the hottest reds, for instance, come from Italy – the square troughs decorated with rosettes and the large pot with decoration around its side, for example. The large containers in the middle of the group are also from Italy. You can buy them in smaller sizes too, which is, perhaps, more convenient for indoor use. The pots from France ornamented with garlands – one is already occupied by a lemon tree on the right, are available in three different sizes.

The large number of flower troughs and other objects in pale colours are Spanish. Those with edges bordered with a plait are simple but decorative and can be found in a number of different shapes and sizes. In the centre there are some hanging or wall pots, the smallest with a scene of dragons, the largest with undulating plant and flower motifs. The one decorated with the head of a lion is particularly beautiful. The little column and the three ribbed melon-shaped pots are also imports from Spain.

Greek earthenware is pale pink in colour, while earthenware which has a powdered finish is made using an ancient technique. Finally, on the extreme left, is an exceptionally elegant urn, while on the right and at the back are a handsome rectangular column and two consoles.

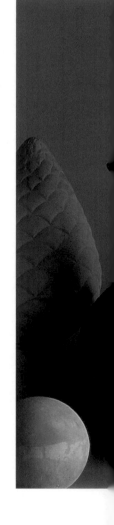

The works shown above are two examples of terracotta wall fountains. The piece with two cherubs, which has a hole for water to spurt out under their feet, comes from Spain and is about fifty years old. The more modern piece, decorated with the face of a young boy surrounded by vines, dribbles water from his mouth.

At the top on the opposite page are some large glazed bowls and a storage jar. These are not necessarily for housing plants – from time to time just a branch or two or some flowers could be placed in them.

The delicate collection of terracotta pieces on the right comes from Spain: a sensual bacchante, a supple looking greyhound (available also in grey), a stylised pine cone and pineapple, and several oval wall plaques. Columns, one of which is lying on its side, are normally composed of four sections. Together they give a total height of 2 metres (6½ ft.), and come in either a smooth or ribbed finish, as you can see on page 85.

On the following pages a selection of decorative vases and garlanded pottery is photographed, in the evening, on my own terrace among plants already well established in pots. Near one of the standard bays with a spiral trunk is the blue silhouette of a shrubby *Plumbago auriculata* in flower, a plant of which I am particularly fond. You can also see two well-rounded crowns of box, two spherical *Eugenia myrtifolia* in urns, an elegant *Citrus aurantium* var. *myrtifolia* and, just by its side, one of two pyramids of climbing plants: passion flower *Passiflora caerulea.*

In the front of the picture are an assortment of wooden water containers, some herbs, an agave and an aloe about which I will write in more detail in the course of the book. Climbing vigorously against the house, the Japanese wisteria (*Wisteria floribunda* 'Longissima alba'), on a wire support, adds touches of white to this green picture. Among the other plants one can also see is the perfumed *Clematis flammula,* the rose 'Rambling Rector' and *Rosa banksiae, Jasminum polyanthum, Clematis alpina* 'White Moth' and, to ensure some winter greenery, honeysuckle (*Lonicera henryi*). Finally, there is *Artemisia stelleriana,* whose soft silvery reflections make a proud contrast to the greenery.

Near the door is an unusual four-handled pot, and a series of straight-sided containers decorated with garlands. These are very practical for repotting newly bought plants from unpleasant black plastic containers. Plants are almost always sold in pots that are too narrow for them, and you will almost certainly need to repot in a size larger (see page 198). The bases of the pottery decorated with lions' heads can be pierced, which gives you the opportunity to use them either as decorative containers or as containers with drainage.

Sometimes old techniques are revived with great success. So it is that today in Frise, north Holland, they are moulding and making bird houses copied from old patterns. The little round pot fixed to the wall of the house between the passion flower and the clematis is the model preferred by sparrows. The example in the form of a sperical pitcher makes a spacious and comfortable nest for starlings. You can also get nests suitable for swallows which you place under the eaves of the roof.

Grey elegance

The many nuances of grey available in earthenware in the fine selection opposite, are due entirely to the sooty smoke of the charcoal given out by the kilns in which the pots are fired. Pots treated in this fashion are coloured right through. The bowl against the wall on the left, the little rectangular trough, and the three decorated pots under the table are the only painted objects, all of them designed and made in Spain. The colour of smoked earthenware depends on its place in the kiln, and when the pot is moistened by earth the tint intensifies. The vivid contrast of the red racemes of *Acalypha hispida* adds a contrast which makes this arrangement a positive delight to the eye.

Faience and white porcelain

As you can see from the colour of the lions' heads and the garlands, the pots on the left hand page have been only partially enamelled.

The French porcelain above comes from the ateliers of Moreau Bourg Joly, one of the rare porcelain artists who has mastered the art of making openwork designs. He concentrates mainly on making faithful copies of old pieces of basketwork. The enamelled terracotta container in the centre is made in Holland, while the two jars in the form of bunches of asparagus come from Italy.

Plants with white flowers obviously look marvellous in these containers, the deep green of their leaves making a good contrast which can be softened by including silvery foliage in the arrangement.

As everybody knows, pots and containers made of enamelled or glazed terracotta or porcelain must be brought indoors without fail before the first frosts appear. It is also recommended that they should not be used for plants if they do not have drainage holes in them, unless they are under a canopy or something similar to keep off the rain. In such conditions you do have some measure of control over the degree of watering. The little ornamental pots have an inner pot of bisque clay inside them in place of drainage holes.

The brilliance of Portuguese pottery

Earthenware in brilliant tints which range from ochre to midnight blue, from cream to bottle green, are welcoming hosts to flowers, plants, leaves and fruits. In the large arrangement below, under the green canopy of a thriving *Radermacheria sinica* (syn. *Sterospermum sinicum*), is a selection

of pots, vases, bowls and dishes which gives colourful evidence of the rich variety of choice offered by Portuguese potteries. The Portuguese tend to rely on making copies of old peasant objects, sometimes in a smaller form, like the blue pot with the small handles which is called 'Don Pedro'.

The collection on the left is all yellow – the yellow of sunflowers in summer. In the jug *Helianthus* *multiflorus* 'Maximus' and *H. anuus* marry well with the golden yellow of the tomatoes, the yellow of the pumpkin and, needless to say, the golden reflections from the Portuguese sunshine.

# HANDSOME SHAPES

Owners of antique pieces can multiply them, if they wish, by making use of copies.

These, when made of long-lasting materials and aged by moss or subjected to the ravages of the weather, make pleasant ornaments for gardens, terraces and balconies.

The column in the illustration on the left has spiral engraving and is topped with a basket of fruit. Copied from an antique English model it is very elegant and very expensive. It is shown, happily, among far less costly and no less stylish articles of garden decoration, which shows that inexpensive items do not have to look vulgar and gaudy, and that just because you don't want to pay much, doesn't mean you have to go for bright colours and bad taste.

The theatrical looking composition below is composed of vases which come from Spain, with the exception of the small bird baths, their borders decorated with a frieze of fruits, which were made in Holland. The vases contain a large papyrus, a fine *Radermacheria sinica* and two vigorous *Carynocarpus laevigatus* with brilliantly shining leaves, the greens of which reflect those of the tiled floor.

CITRUS TREES

The many varieties of citrus tend to give their owners an irrespressible desire to become serious collectors and to gather together large numbers of these plants whose elegance is only exceeded by the succulence of their fruits. The search for species can become a passionate hobby which can give you unforgettable moments.

Citrus plants thrive particularly well if they are not placed too near other plants and if they are kept free from pests. Their culture is relatively simple, considering the fact that the aim of the horticulturist is to transform as many flowers as possible into fruits. With this in mind, the application of fertiliser should always be carried out with discretion: a fertiliser high in nitrogen, for instance, will encourage the development of leaves to the detriment of flowers and fruit.

These two pages show us two ways of using citrus trees. One is in a winter garden – an orangery (left), with the tree growing in a superb pot made in Italy in 1810, the other is in the form of a summer line-up with the trees planted in traditional Versailles tubs. This last picture shows them perfectly placed to make a rhythmic composition.

The forty year old lemon tree (above) is kept mainly for utilitarian purposes and is the star attraction of a collection of citrus. A year and a half before this old tree was transplanted, it was root-pruned by ringing it with a deep trench which was then refilled with fresh humus. New hair roots developed which were carefully freed during the transfer to a new pot. To lighten the task of the root system which had been reduced, the healthy foliage had to be cut back severely – almost pollarded. The large older branches form the base for the new wood which makes all the top growth of the tree. Although expensive, these citrus trees are well worth every penny.

On the opposite page a pair of small citrus trees stand either side of a magnificent garden table. Its blue stone top stands on two plinths, cement reproductions of Louis XV pedestals. The dragons are part of a cast-iron bench made around 1910.

A catalogue for collectors

The list which follows is given for the benefit of citrus enthusiasts. Apart from listing the popular name of the species and the hybrids we also give, wherever possible, the scientific name. Personally I cannot help finding a certain quaint charm in these double descriptions.

Citrus amblyocarpa. The fruits, heavily wrinkled and acid yellow, are much sought after by Indonesian cooks.

Citrus aurantifolia. Like the lime in that its fruits are bright green; it has a more strongly perfumed juice than most lemons.

Citrus aurantium. The Seville orange; this is the bitter orange that is used to make marmalade.

Citrus aurantium ssp. *amara.* Produces a kind of bitter orange which is much appreciated by the Japanese.

Citrus aurantium var. *myrtifolia.* With small foliage, similar to that of a myrtle, it produces flattish oranges with a bitter taste (see pages 39 and 41).

Citrus bergamia. The flesh of these non-edible fruits produces an essence which is used in the making of eau de Cologne.

Citrus bigaradia 'Sinensis'. The Chinese bitter orange.The flowers of this old species produce essence of neroli which is used in perfumes. The fruits are used widely in the making of marmalades, jams, liqueurs and medicines.

Citrus bigaradia 'Violacea'. Another variety of Seville orange. It is, however, almost impossible to obtain fruit from this species.

Citrus deliciosa. A mandarin which has been hybridised to produce fruits which are sometimes called Tangier oranges or tangerines.

Citrus grandis (syn. *C. maxima*) The scientific name for the grapefruit.

Citrus hystrix. The fruits of this little known tree are called papedas.

Citrus limetta (syn. *C. limonia* var.

limetta) produces smooth lemons.

Citrus limon. The common lemon.

Citrus medica. The true citrus, used in cake making and perfumery.

Citrus medica var. *chirocarpus* (syn. *C. medica* var. *sarcodactylis*). Originating from Japan, the busho-kan or 'Buddha's finger' produces long oval fruits.

Citrus 'Meyer's Lemon'. The result of a cross between *C. limon* and *Poncirus trifoliata* (the old *C.*

trifoliata), this tree is very resistant to cold and survives the rigours of the northern European climate without any problems.

Citrus microcarpa. Imported from the Philippines in 1595, this tree produces tiny very acid fruits which are also very aromatic. Called *calamansis* in the Philippines, it is also known as the calamondin orange.

Citrus mitis produces tiny non-edible orange fruits and is usually grown as an indoor plant.

Citrus x *nobilis* is the result of a cross between *C. grandis* and *C. reticulata,* and produces royal oranges.

Citrus otaitensis is also known as *C.* x *limonia* because it results from a cross between *C. limon* and *C. reticulata.*

Citrus paradisi is the scientific name of the grapefruit or pomelo.

Citrus paradisi x *C. deliciosa*. This large succulent fruit, the result of crossing a grapefruit with a tangerine, looks rather unattractive and is therefore popularly known as the 'ugli' fruit.

Citrus reticulata. A similar variety to the crossing which produces mandarin oranges.

Citrus reticulata x *C. paradisi* produces a hybrid fruit known as a tangelo.

Citrus sinensis is the common orange and was once known as the apple of China. This explains its qualification 'sinensis' – Chinese.

Citrus sinensis x *C. deliciosa*. The cross of an orange and a tangerine, the fruit of this tree is called the ortanique.

Citrus sinensis x *C. limon*. This hybrid produces a fruit called citrange.

Citrus sinensis x *C. reticulata*. The cross of an orange and a mandarin, the fruit is called malaquina.

Citrus sinensis 'Variegatus'. The fruit of this variety with multi-coloured leaves is sometimes called the pineapple orange.

Fortunella margarita. Resembling a small very aromatic orange, the fruit of the kumquat is usually eaten in syrup or jam.

Fortunella margarita x citrange produces fruits called the citrangequat.

Fortunella margarita x *C. aurantifolia* produces the limquat which possesses flesh as acid as the lemon.

Fortunella margarita x *C. limon*. A cross producing fruits called lemonquats.

Fortunella margarita x *C. sinensis* is a hybrid producing orangequats.

Poncirus trifoliata. A variety with sharp spines capable of resisting the rigours of northern winters. However, the small yellow fruits are not edible.

The *Citrus limon,* the true lemon, comes just behind the grapefruit and *C. medica* on the scale of citrus trees which produce an abundance of flowers. The petals of its perfumed blooms have edges tinged with rose-purple. In our experience the fruit does not attain maturity for two years, and should be left on the tree to ripen so that you get fruit and flowers side by side on the same plant, as you can see in the photograph on the right.

Below, a classic composition of citrus plants in terracotta pots. On the far right a lemon tree sends out its perfume for the benefit of anyone who sits in one of the seats in the inner courtyard of a chateau. Cut in fine grain stone, the table comes from Italy where it was made at the turn of the 17th and 18th century. Modern copies are now on sale, however, in garden centres.

Whatever type of citrus tree you buy, it is important to make sure that it is sold in a pot which contains the right soil. In effect, citrus trees appreciate more than anything else a rich heavy well firmed soil. You can now buy commercially prepared compost that is specially appropriate for these trees which makes things much easier.

SUCCULENT PLANTS

The word succulent covers a large number of plants which only need little care and are easy to cultivate in a pot. With succulents the daily watering routine no longer applies. Adapted as they are to desert or near desert conditions in their natural environment, they hoard moisture and food in their thick fleshy leaves during the rare periods of rainfall which are separated by long periods of drought.

A large number of succulents can be kept indoors, so for most of the year I keep the collection shown on the left under cover. One of the reasons I bought the wrought-iron chair dating from around 1835 was to show off the collection. The tubs of thick wood made in India in the 19th century in which some of my succulents are housed cannot cope with alternate humidity and drought, and this explains the choice of succulents for them as these don't need a lot of water.

The largest of the containers houses a red-leaved stonecrop (*Sedum rubrotinctum* 'Aurore'), while its shorter neighbour shows off the rounded fat bowl-like leaves of *An-dromischus,* which goes under the name of 'plovers eggs' in Great Britain. The smallest pot houses the blue-tinged sugar almond plant, *Pachyphytum oviferum.* Under the seat is the fragile *Pilea microphylla.* A *Rhipsalis mesembryan-themoides* nestles in one of the hardwood tubs, and behind it, in the larger one, is a coral cactus pompously called *Hatiora salicornioides.*

Above, a multitude of silver rosettes of x *Graptoveria* 'Calva' housed in a number of different containers makes a splendid but delicate contrast to the robust *Hosta* and the lacy leaves of ferns. The x *Graptoveria* is the result of a cross between a *Graptopetalum* and an *Echeveria,* and the term 'calva' refers to its nut colour. Succulent enthusiasts should definitely visit botanic gardens and other places where they can see plants growing in ideal conditions in all their diverse colours.

Rosettes in harmony

In summer the colours of rosette-shaped succulents come almost entirely from their leaves, and although their flowers are attractive, they are by no means indispensable.

The centre of the picture is dominated by an *Echevaria glauca* (the qualification refers to the blue tone of the rosettes). This succulent grows very easily and quickly produces a multitude of offsets which almost overflow from the container. Like other plants of the group, echeveria must be transferred indoors in winter, where it needs to be placed in a spot that is as well lit as possible (in contrast, the robust nature of box means it can be left out of doors).

In the main growing season the stiff flowers shoot up in a firework display of pinks and yellows which does not die down for several weeks, and the colours remain pleasing until the moment comes to cut them down.

Echeveria 'Perle von Nürnberg' develops in a different way. Its purple rosettes do not produce smaller offspring, but it is very easy to take cuttings. Just take one leaf or a mini rosette and plant it in a pot filled with sandy soil.

On the left of the picture a young *Haworthia attenuata* var. *caespitosa* perches on the petrified sweetmeats in the front of the picture. A good assortment of young succulents can be found in most florists these days.

The houseleek, *Sempervivum tectorum,* makes itself at home with ease in the most unlikely containers as you can see from the examples here. The hanging terracotta vase (right) was given to me by a friend, and although it is most elegant it is unhappily unable to accommodate plants with vigorous roots which need a lot of soil. But the sempervivum took it over without any problems and now covers the surface with its thick cushions. Its container hangs just below the ripening pears on one of the trees in the small orchard on my terrace. This pear is also host to another guest, a *Clematis orientalis* whose tendrils mix with its lovely feathery seed heads.

The extraordinary facility of hybrids of the houseleek to adapt to any situation is perfectly illustrated by the occupants of two stone baptismal fonts which serve as temporary outlets for water which flows off the thatched roof of my house (far right). In effect, the houseleek seems to make mock of excessive watering. The tendrils of *Clematis fargesii* and *Passiflora caerulea* entwine and mesh with each other around the font.

Unlike *Clematis fargesii,* passion flowers cannot survive the rigours of a really hard winter. If they are taken down from their support and curled up on the ground, the stems can be protected with a thick covering of straw – which is a better alternative to having dead leaves on the trellis.

The large picture on the far right features another hardy succulent with the evocative name of *Sempervivella alba.* The Latin words *semper* – (always) and *vivum* – (living) appear, in fact, in the names of many plants which have the characteristic of being able to resist winter frosts, and the succulents mentioned on this page can live outside all the year.

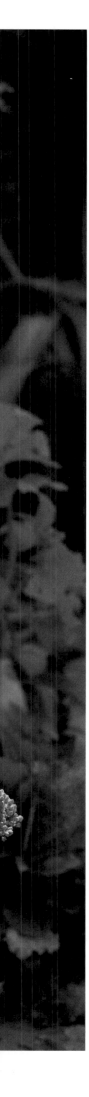

Flowering festoons

The combination of rosette-shaped plants and some of the innumerable species of succulents are infinite as well as being infinitely seductive. The page opposite illustrates the elegance of the trailing *Sedum sieboldii* 'Variegatum'. At the end of the summer, clear pink edges appear at the end of its branches. Generally classed as an indoor plant, it nevertheless puts up well with the most rigorous frosts. At the foot of this page, the woolly rosy flowers of *Orostachys aggregatus* is sprinkled with little white-green florets. As it is incapable of surviving the more severe frosts, it is important to bring this species indoors for the worst weeks of winter.

Appreciating open ground as well as space in a pot, *Sedum spectabile,* which is irresistible to butterflies in the warmth of the autumn sun, dominates the left hand corner of the picture on the right. On the table is a *Sedum sieboldii* with single coloured flowers which explains the absence of the term *variegatum* in its scientific name.

Some Portuguese immigrants

The azure blue container below comes from Portugal, as do those in the photographs on the right-hand page. And many of the plants that grow in Portugal, even though it is situated further south, can be grown in northern Europe if you are prepared to take them indoors during the winter.

Aeonium arboreum (left) is one of the easiest Portuguese plants to cultivate; the smallest cutting put in sandy soil will be sure to grow. It can be bought in most florists. The qualification *arboreum* indicates that the plant takes on a tree-like tendency after several years. Many hybrids only produce their rosettes in the spring, others are permanently covered in tints of brown or purple.

Aeonium holochrysum (top right) offers a completely different look. Its branches of rosettes produce elegant tips of bright yellow flowers grouped together in miniature peaks.

Although less spectacular, the lampranthus at the foot of the facing page is, nevertheless, very pleasant to look at. The blue-green of its foliage mixes with the lilac-rose of its flowers. It shares a similar parent to mesembryanthemum which we normally cultivate as an annual plant. Few people know, by the way, that one of these varieties is perfectly edible. Covered with little transparent 'glands' with a frosted appearance, *Mesembryanthemum crystallum* can be cooked and eaten like spinach. You may be able to track it down in top quality vegetable shops and herb farms on the Continent.

People who live in Mediterranean regions have no difficulty in raising agaves, aloes and other succulents, unlike those from the north who are forced to take them inside over winter. All the same, they demand a minimum of attention and give an extremely exotic look with their vigorous rosettes with sharp pointed leaves. Their distinctive leaf shapes make a pleaing contrast to other vegetation, as you can see on pages 41 and 76.

If you are buying these particular plants, however, you need to take certain precautions. The containers in which they are sometimes sold often do not have drainage holes, and this can have disastrous consequences if the plants are left out in the rain, when they will quickly rot. So it is important either to make a hole in the bottom of the pot or put the plant in another container with adequate drainage. As a general rule, plants that you buy should almost always be repotted because very often their roots have completely filled the container. To avoid damaging or cutting the roots when carrying out this operation, it is necessary to moisten the soil well and tap the pot firmly on the side to loosen the soil. In the case of a plastic pot, it's enough simply to squeeze the pot in your hand so that the plant comes out. Aeonium and agaves should be repotted into a special cactus compost. Aloes also appreciate compost that is mixed with a little sand for drainage.

Clustered beside the doorway of the house (below right) a shiny blue pot holds the vigorous blue rosettes of *Agave attenuata* and the smaller leaves of *Aloe stricta* with rosy pink floral shafts. In a large tub on the extreme right, a clump of stag's horn shaped *Aloe arborescens* opens up its thrusting leaves. In front of them are the blue rosettes of *Aeonium haworthii,* planted here in the ground but often grown in pots.

The group of plants (below) is dominated by a sky-blue pot in which is planted a spectacular *Aeonium cuneatum.* The round bellied pot with handles provides an ideal container for the *Crassula ovata* 'Frutescens', while a group of aloes cascades in front of the window. At the front is a bed carpeted with *Mesembryanthemum rosens,* a near relative of the lampranthus shown on the preceding page. On the right hand page, the intense blue foliage of a *Dudleya pulverulenta* is spiked with the white of its flowering peduncles.

NATURAL GROWTH

Earthenware vases and pots are not always necessary to obtain spectacular effects. Plants can grow in other places. Stone and concrete can become covered in moss, for instance, and small plants can establish themselves on roof tiles or in niches in a wall. Even the branches of a tree can give support to climbing plants.

The balustrade and stone containers (left) have been covered with an attractive incrustation of lichens which are, nevertheless, extremely damaging. This water garden is in a celebrated late 17th, early 18th century Portuguese estate. The urns are planted with *Pelargonium peltatum.*

In hot climates certain kinds of succulents grow spontaneously on roofs, and in the illustration below a *Sedum* has taken firm control.

The wall as a container

It sometimes happens that, in the case of old crumbling walls, the masonry all but disappears under exuberant vegetation. Plants will frequently seed in niches and produce miniscule plants (miniscule because, growing as they do in cracks in the wall, they lack nutrition). In order to transform a wall into a perfect supporting structure for plants like the one on the left, give it a helping hand: put in small rampant plants like *Cymbalaria muralis,* the climbing *Lobelia erinus* and other fast-growing annuals. Try a planting of lady's mantle (*Alchemilla mollis*) and see how rapidly it multiplies, setting off the wall with its leaves which every morning have drops of dew like pearls in their centres.

The tree as a support

Grow some plants up a tree, or perhaps even a pole, and climbers will transform the saddest bundle of sticks into into bushes verdant with leaves and flowers. The most simple plant to use is ivy (*Hedera helix*) which clings to the trunk of a tree without aid, and eventually spreads its garlands out along the branches (see left).

Roses are also marvellous in trees – think of *Rosa filipes* 'Kiftsgate' which dangles it rose-perfumed boughs from stems as much as 20 metres (65½ ft.) long. Equally beautiful are some varieties of clematis, honeysuckle (varieties of *Lonicera* can withstand a great deal of shade) and climbing hydrangeas, whose scientific name is *Hydrangea anomala* spp. *petiolaris.*

The roof as a garden

Natural vegetation manifests itself particularly on old roofs (above). The vagaries of wind and climate in time may deposit little leaves in cracks in the tiles which, over the years, become humus in which seeds can plant themselves. If you want to help nature with this work, a thin covering of soil, kept in place by fine chickenwire or something similar is a good idea. Little ferns, *Cymbalaria muralis* and Corsican mint (*Mentha requienii*) will develop very quickly in this environment. Above all don't choose the type of mint used for cooking or other wild plants will be overwhelmed by its rampaging roots. They would also displace the tiles in your roof and encourage leaks.

71

WOODEN CONTAINERS

By its very nature wood goes perfectly with leaves and flowers. Made originally to hold liquids, barrels and butts make equally good receptacles both for aquatic plants and those planted in soil. A simple wooden container, by itself or near water, makes a simple but perfect decoration for a conservatory.

The large cupboard on the left is used to house garden utensils. Don't worry at all if you inadvertently drench furniture like this when watering plants.

Miniature trees of *Chrysanthemum frutescens* prefer to overwinter in a constant ambient temperature of 7-10 degrees celsius (44.5-50 degrees fahrenheit), with just enough water to keep their foliage going through the season without shrivelling. I have used this method for several years now and have watched their little trunks become better and thicker each year.

On the right, beside a 17th century chest, a 19th century Japanese tub houses a *Plectranthus fruticosus*.

On this and the following pages you will see that is is not possible to grow plants which demand a great deal of water in wooden containers unless they are wooden barrels made with staves which can contract in dry conditions or swell in a humid atmosphere. This is why pots in hollowed out solid wood are only used for the culture of succulents which need just a small amount of water.

The elegant tub on the left houses a miniature box tree which is complemented by a bed of ivy. The small oval leaves of *Buxus sempervirens* contrast admirably with the large shiny leaves of the different climbing ivies (*Hedera helix*). On the right, in a tub filled with annuals is a climbing species – canary creeper (*Tropaeolum peregrinum*), whose stems range in all directions seeking something on which to attach themselves. Forget-me-not is also flowering in the tub, together with a variety of the annual *Chrysanthemum parthenium* 'Roya'.

At the back of the picture, tall spires of verbascum can be seen cultivated in open ground together with mallow (*Malva mauritiana*) with its deep violet-red flowers.

In the gardens at Priona (left), an imposing collection of white mulleins (*Verbascum thapsus*) is set off by a fascinating group of plants in pots. At the front, a tub made from rings of bark is mainly filled with pinks (*Dianthus deltoides*). At its side is a large flowerpot containing scented rosemary (*Rosmarinus officinalis*), while a magnificent example of one of the many species of aloes adds to the scene, all these cultivated outside in a courtyard in summer. On the top of the wall to the right, *Crambe cordifolia* showers down its clouds of tiny white flowers, while the *Hieracium caespitosum* with its yellow blooms testifies to the fact that a number of wild plants are also grown in this garden.

Top right, a little washtub shelters a small collection of carnivorous plants among which is a *Drosera* with small long hairy tentacles (*D. longifolia*), a purple *Sarracenia purpurea* with leaves curled into cornets – veritable insect traps, while, at the back of the tub, the long graceful red-tipped stems of *S. oreophila* fan out. As soon as the first night frosts threaten these plants must be brought in and put in a bright place with a temperature of around 7 degrees celsius (44.5 degrees fahrenheit).

In principal, the sundew (*Drosera*), which can sometimes be found in its wild state, is a hardy perennial, but the examples that are on sale in spring in garden centres and florists have been subjected to intensive culture and because of that they should be treated in the same way as other carnivorous plants, and this goes for small subtropical aquatics purchased at the same time.

Below right, an elegant small banded wooden tub contains the coral cactus (*Hatiora salicornioides*) which is perfectly happy out in the open in the summer, despite the fact that it comes from Brazil.

WATER GARDENS

In this chapter I hope I will be able to convince the reader that the culture of aquatic plants in a vat or barrel is more than just an attractive occupation. A large pond, where it is pleasant to linger in summer, is a feature of my garden: aquatic plants abound and attract many frogs as well as dragonflies which dip and soar as they escape attacks by swallows.

To tell the truth I am still researching which plants are perennial and which are not in such containers. This is in order to advise people who have only got a small garden or just a balcony. What is so good about these aquatic gardens, however, is that you get so much immediate pleasure from them compared with a pond at the bottom of the garden. In the morning you can drink your cup of coffee beside them, or stand there in the twilight with a glass in your hand. You appreciate their perfume, and continually congratulate yourself for having made such a wise decision! And what enchantment there is in May when everything is in flower, springing up from water that not so long ago was a block of ice!

On frost

In the course of the years I have found that waterlilies (*Nymphaea*) in shallow tubs or barrels sawn in half tend to freeze when the winter is hard. The waterlilies illustrated on page 78 have survived two rigorous winters in their tall barrel. When winters are mild, however, these plants can equally well exist in shallow tubs.

Nevertheless, whatever the type of tub, it is vital to make a hole in the ice when it freezes. I do this with the aid of a kitchen chopper, and in the case of hard frosts I have to hit the ice really hard before I reach water. In some temperatures the ice may crack easily, spurting out a veritable geyser at the first tap. If this operation is not done daily and most of the water turns into ice, your barrel will really be under pressure. This small daily chore could be made easier, perhaps, by using a defrosting agent instead.

On waterlilies

Choose varieties of waterlilies which are suggested for a depth of 30 to 100cm (12-39½ ins.) when you are growing them in tall tubs. The *Nymphaea* x *marliacea* 'Carnea', for instance, with its pretty pink flowers, or *N. odorata* 'Alba', which is white and perfumed, are both shown on the previous page.

Then, floating elegantly in their troughs, the water lettuce (*Pistia stratiotes*), the little waterlily *Hydrocharis morsus-ranae*, and *Myriophyllum aquaticum* (syn. *M. proserpinacoides*), all grow in a charmingly disordered fashion.

Above left is one of my favourite plants in the world of water culture, *Menyanthes trifoliata* with its sweet perfume. The same barrel shelters a large number of *Calla palustris* whose pretty berries on long stems can be seen on page 155.

species which is not hardy but very pretty – the little waterlily *Nymphaea pygmaea* 'Helvola'. Beside this tender yellow variety is a *N. pygmaea* 'Alba' which produces seeds, though 'Helvola' doesn't.

During spring and summer *Pistia stratiotes* and the little floating plant *Salvinia natans* multiply. At the beginning of each year I buy them and water hyacincths which I plant out in all my tubs.

On soil and fertiliser

Naturally you can mix the necessary soil yourself, but I personally prefer to buy bags containing special ready-prepared soil which you can find in most garden centres. One bag is enough for a small tub, larger ones need two or three bags. In the smallest containers, if you are cultivating marginal or bog plants, you will need plenty of soil. These plants need about 12cm (4¾ ins.) of water. Your bowls of aquatic plants should never be fertilised; indeed you don't put fertiliser in a pond. One exception, however, is if you are cultivating the lotus, for the Indian lotus (*Nelumbo nucifera*) thrives better in a compost composed of a quarter of fresh soil and three quarters of well rotted compost.

On mud-filled containers

The mud-filled containers in which I cultivate bog plants are not shown here. These plants include, for example, the water mint (*Mentha aquatica*) which is very pleasant to find on on a terrace where you can run your hand over its perfumed foliage. I also love to grow *Geum rivale* because I love the shape of its leaves (see one in flower on page 99). And in very large, very solid casks I grow *Gunnera manicata* with its huge rhubarb-like leaves (far right in the large illustration). If a sharp frost is expected the casks should be protected by straw.

On the far left is a Lilliputian water world, a mixture of plants contrasting sharply with the aloe and the agave alongside them. In the bowl are *Hippuris vulgaris* with *Potentilla palustre,* the arrow-like *Sagittaria sagittifolia* and the white form of *Caltha palustris.* In the centre is the water hyacinth *Eichhornia crassipes* which doesn't develop its magnificent blue flowers unless the summers are very hot, but multiplies ferociously whatever the weather.

Pictured above is my pride and joy, a small vat which contains a

DATURAS

brings a glimmer of pleasure to the eyes of enthusiasts.

The title of this chapter is, in fact, inappropriate: the vast majority of these attractive perfumed plants have in effect recovered their old name of Brugmansia *which will eventually be given to all of them, but meanwhile* Datura *is a more familiar name and one which*

The large photograph on the right illustrates a perfect combination of the double white angels' trumpets of *Brugmansia suaveolens* 'Knightii' with other white flowers.

A basket-patterned pot filled with *Hymenocallis* x *festalis* enriches the range of perfumes in the group. This plant is the result of a cross between *Elisena longipetala* and *Hymenocallis calathina* and has until now sold under the name of *Ismene festalis*.

The Californian eschscholtzias (*Eschscholtzia californica* 'Milky White') in their creamy tones (far right) add to the silent concert of trumpets which dominates them.

Behind the pot of *Brugmansia,* on a little bank, is a pot of anemones de Caen and another rounded pot which shelters the roots of *Gaura lindheimeri,* a plant which will flower again in November (this photograph was taken in early July).

These lovely perfumed plants diffuse their scents on a parterre of modest meadow rue (*Thalictrum dioicum*) with yellow green calyxes and purple stamens.

There are other hybrid forms of *Brugmansia* which are equally exciting: *Brugmansia* x *insignis* 'Pink', with colours that run the gamut of pinks from rose to salmon, and *B. insignis* 'Orange' with golden flowers with satiny reflections.

Introduced for the first time in England in 1845, the slender lemon-yellow bells of *Datura chlorantha* are seldom if ever seen. These plants, with their fresh young perfume, are never found except in the most stately gardens. And although *Brugmansia sanguinea* is, unfortunely unscented, it is always possible to cheat on that score, bearing in mind its wonderful palette of colours (see page 6).

The two small photographs on the left show two forms of *Datura metel,* an annual, proudly bearing its trumpets with pleated centres. The flowers are purple and white shades, and the fruits, prickly apples, are sometimes full of seeds.

The enthusiast who likes a wide ranging palette of colours will be interested to hear of the *Iochroma* species. Members of the *Solanaceae* family, and in the same group as *Daturas* and *Brugmansias,* to which they are closely related, these plants produce smaller flowers some 8cm (3ins.) long and 3cm (1¼ins.) in diameter at the back.

While the flowers of *Iochroma cyneum* 'Indigo' are a beautiful blue-violet colour, those of *I. cyaneum* 'Sky King' are a dazzling sky-blue. Those of *I. fuchsioides* span the orange tones, while the largest, those of *I. grandiflora,* are also tinged with blue.

 # SUMMER BULBS

A surprisingly large number of varieties of summer flowering bulbs can be grown in the confined space of a container. Happily, too, for most of these plants cannot resist the rigours of our winters. Put in pots, on the other hand, they can always be brought indoors to a cool dark place where they will overwinter comfortably.

In the large group on the right are two pots of *Acidanthera bicolor* which have not yet flowered, a cord-decorated pot which houses two *Ornithogalum arabicum,* and another in the shape of a pumpkin from which a single white tubular *Agapanthus* grows. On the ground is a pot completely filled with *Oxalis regnellii.*

In addition to this, on the table is the scented-leaved geranium, *Pelargonium tomentosum,* its furry leaves strongly scented with mint, which has, over the years, grown very large. There is also a *Brugmansia sanguinea* which is not yet in flower. By the column in the left of the picture is a pot with another scented geranium, *Pelargonium odoratissimum.* A spherical vase contains a little trailing violet which flowers right up to the first night frosts. This also has to be brought in in winter to shelter from the cold. The silvery cactus on the right of the table is *Astrophytum myriostigma.*

From time to time you find lilies on sale that have been specially bred for culture in pots. These are, for example, short stemmed hybrids like 'Peach Blush', 'Liberation' and 'Sterling Star'. The heavily scented *Lilium longiflorum* is not hardy but is sold in its thousands as a cut flower. For a year or two now it has also made an appearance as a pot plant. The three bulbs that I have grown in pots have done remarkably well (page 93). Encouraged by their success I have continued to cultivate many more lilies in pots. Most of the hybrids have done astonishingly well, as you can see from the orange-red group opposite. In pursuing my studies with a mix of 'Aurelian' hybrids, I've tended to pot the bulbs separately as I do not like a mix of different colours. So far my experiment has been crowned with success. However, my tentative attempts to grow *Lilium tenuifolium* have ended in failure, although *L. henryi* (opposite top) has done very well in pots despite being put in a narrow rather shady spot. However, as you can see, the stems of the lilies lean towards the light.

This group receives its perfume from *Acidanthera bicolor,* visible at the back of the picture, and the ravishing little shoots of *Trachelospermum jasminoides.* These little perfumed white flowers and their shiny leaves are also visible on the extreme right on page 78. In the front of the picture a shallow jar shows off the beautiful summer turquoise of *Euphorbia myrsinites* which produces yellow-green flowers in the spring. Always try to complete your groupings with little details – here the intense turquoise blue of the succulent, there the white of a *Cymbalaria muralis* 'Alba'.

During the summer all shades of amaryllis (*Hippeastrum*) can be grouped together with other plants, as in the bottom illustration on the opposite page. There is also a small plant now available that is a remarkable cross between a *Hippeastrum* and a *Sprekelia,* developing shafts of flowers from bulbs. It is called *Hippeastralia* 'Tub's Beauty'.

If you particularly prize pink tints, then look for the varieties of Japanese lily (*Lilium speciosum*). On page 122 half hidden among the leaves of the elegant *Albizia* is a long narrow trough filled with *Lilium speciosum* 'Uchida Kanoka'.

Round ornamented pots containing *Amaryllis belladonna* in pale pink tints make a very special effect. And if you have a sufficiently deep container, then several *Crinum* x *powellii* are well worth growing. When cultivated in pots they must be brought in to shelter from frost. The exception to this rule is *Lilium longiflorum*, which can stay out of doors throughout the cold season.

The illustration on the right shows a splendid display of *Eucomis bicolor*. These are not expensive and three bulbs are enough to make a good-looking display. They will flower each year as long as you keep them protected from frost.

At the bottom of this page on the left, is a variety of *Eucomis* that comes in pastel tones: the flowers of *E. punctata* are mainly confined to pink and cream. Much later the white *E. autumnalis* appears, while each bulb of *E. zambesica* produces three or four spikes of ravishing green flowers.

In contrast one cannot but admire the fireworks of *Acidanthera bicolor* (left). As they are very cheap, the small bulbs can be planted in groups of twenty or more in the same container. It's a good idea, however, to repeat this operation at three weekly intervals, as the vanilla-scented flowers don't last more than six weeks, and by planting in succession it is possible to extend the flowering season.

The superb specimen of *Begonia* x *tuberhybrida pendula* 'White Cascade' below shows what a splendid display can be obtained from the most humble of flowers.

Another lovely summer flowering bulb is *Ornithogalum arabicum* – 'une perle noire'. The pearly centre of this plant gives off a lemon scent with a hint of cinnamon. This variety unfortunately loses its scent quickly when it is sold as a cut flower.

Once sold under the name of *Ismene festalis*, the fantastic *Hymenocallis* x *festalis* (see page 83) is easy to grow in a cool shady place.

For the purposes of this book I also started to grow *Galtonia candicans* in a pot, that is, the varieties with white flowers that are easily available at the moment. The perfect result of these tentative experiments can be seen in the centre of the photograph on page 94.

The perfume enthusiast is bound to turn, sooner or later, to growing *Polianthes tuberosa*. The powerful penetrating scent of the tuberose is not guaranteed every year – at least not in the case of the specimens I have grown. It is inconvenient to try to cover them with straw in the winter if they are kept in containers. Better to buy a large number of bulbs and grow them in a sunny spot.

FROM ORANGE TO RED

Arrangements based on orange and red can be among the most spectacular of all, but they need a special touch. Nature, the artist, has her own talent for this risky exercise as the hibiscus on this page bears witness.

The handsome hibiscus is an aristocrat of the plant world. Pompously christened *Hibiscus sinensis* hybrid 'Charles Schmidt', the species below right was voted hibiscus of the year in 1985 in the U.S.A. The last few years have seen a rise in popularity of this plant which belongs to the *Malvaceae* family. Whether a tender rose-pink, a vivid yellow or pale cream, the flower tones of this plant are some of the prettiest notes in the plant symphony.

Included with the hibiscus is a small trailing species which tends to hide the beauty of its flowers, but the detail (above) reveals the resplendent colours of *Fuchsia procumbens* whose flowers never really reach more than 2cm (¾ in.) long. Each year these strange lanterns are replaced by edible red berries, a delicacy much enjoyed by the Maoris in New Zealand. This plant has no chance of surviving the winter in open ground.

Another of the brilliant summer bulbs is shown left. *Haemanthus multiflorus* flowers in April/May on a bare stem, coming before the superb crown of flowers of *H. katherinae*, a species with particularly long stalks which appears in July/August.

The spectacular firework display on the far right is created by oranges and yellows in an orange pot decorated with a knotted garland. Behind it a portrait by Corstiaan de Vries of one of his two daughters. The palette and form of this display is echoed by the *Azalea japonica* in the niche (right). After flowering, put azaleas out in open ground in a shady spot during the summer and fertilise well. In that way you will be sure of abundant flowers the following year.

HITE

White flowers bloom throughout the seasons and are yet another feature in the range of infinite possibilities offered by growing plants in pots. The delicate charm of spring blooms gives way to the exuberance of summer species clothed in white which fade with the end of summer. The examples here will, I hope, encourage you to try new arrangements.

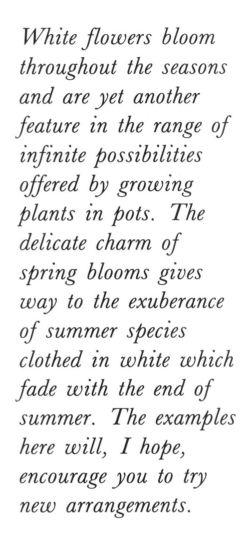

The flowers of the elegant tulips 'Court Lady' (below left), tower majestically above a carpet of forget-me-nots (*Myosotis*) and pansies. This form of white bloom, *Tulipa viridiflora,* is one of the oldest and most attractive. The bulbs, which are easy to cultivate, can be dried off and stored after flowering. The photograph above transports the enthusiast to the sophisticated world of *Hymenocallis* x *macrostephana* with its vanilla scent.

The illustration on the right shows a lovely spring group. The buds of three *Lilium longiflorum* droop over their terracotta pot, while on the right at the back is the long-flowering *Nierembergia frutescens* 'White Queen'.

The arrangement (on page 93) is bisected by a white *Dicentra spectabilis* 'Alba'. The huge shell, *Tridacna gigas,* will resist even the coldest winters and has been used as a bird bath in my garden for several years.

Cultivated in a pot, the *Galtonia candicans* (left), shows off all its natural assets, its elegant scented bells dominating the other plants in this arrangement. Equally happy in spacious containers, *Delphinium* x *cultorum* 'Ivory Towers' makes a luminous contrast to *Astilbe* x *arendsii* 'Brautschleier'. Turning to a slight pink tint at the end of the season, the white flower clusters of *Hydrangea paniculata* die off about the same time as the capsules of the *Galtonia.* At the left near a small *Myrtus communis,* a lemon-scented *Pelargonium* gives a touch of perfume to this plant composition; on the right is an orange tree, *Citrus sinensis* 'Washington Naval'.

Full of symbols and traditions, the myrtle produces perfumed flowers with powder-puff stamens (small illustration, left). *Papaver somnifera* 'Cream Paeony' (small illustration, right) is only a modest height when it is cultivated in a pot, which makes it all the more charming; thrusting deep into the soil, its wide ranging roots need a deep container *Viburnum plicatum* 'Mariesii' tends to develop horizontally. It adapts very well to large pots and to roof gardens like the one shown on the right.

The starry flowered chrysanthemum can be found in many forms, though not all of them are resistant to cold and these must be brought in as soon as the first signs of frost appear. A little care and attention will give them the chance to flower again the following year though not always quite so vigorously, for these plants are often forced by horticulturists and become exhausted by accelerated growth. Left, a gracious sculptured vase houses the late-flowering chrysanthemum 'Bronze Elegans' which is capable of surviving the hardest winters. On the left of the picture are the large leaves of a hollyhock (*Althaea rosea*). Put quite by chance into a container meant for hostas, it now makes a particularly decorative feature in the garden. The plump rosettes belong to a succulent, one of the *Aeoniums*.

Right, a sumptuous floral arrangement designed by Walda Pairon to decorate her garden for an autumn fête. The white Ethiopian arums (*Zantedeschia aethiopica*) are interspersed among a mosaic of *Delphinium* x *cultorum* and *Ammi majus*. The stone vases were made in France around 1880. In the background you can just see the top of a garden seat — a famous design by Sir Edwin Lutyens. The table is carved from a massive piece of oak and is capable of resisting strong variations in humidity.

YELLOW HUES

Whether they are creamy, bright, sharp or intense, yellows always create combinations which are fresh and gay. *In spring when the light is still weak the pale tones are marvellous, but when summer arrives they become hotter and brighter.*

For spring I have chosen tones of creamy yellow (near left) which harmonise perfectly with the colour of the large pale pot which contains a broom, *Cytisus* x *praecox.* The same goes for the oval container full of cream-coloured poppies, a mix of *Papaver nudicaule* 'Cream Shades'. The wooden sections of this container were not watertight when I bought it but have swollen after a damp summer when I put aquatic plants in it.

I always choose *Aquilegia vulgaris* 'Beidermeier' for this springtime ensemble and a greenish-flowered form of *Geum rivale* 'Album' which stays pretty long after its pendulous flowers have gone, being superseded by fluffy fruits. And among the silvery foliage of the broom I have planted, for one summer at any rate, a lily, 'Sterling Star', which unfortunately, cannot be seen in the photograph.

On the far left is one of the many attractive varieties of *Abutilon* which can actually be grown from cuttings or seed. This one with yellow flowers and orange centres is *Abutilon* hybrid 'Moonchimes', but you can also find varieties in pale pink. You can buy innumerable forms of *Abutilon megapontanicum* and *A. pictum* (syn. *striatum*): their flowers are plain yellow or prettily veined with tones of pink and orange. *Abutilon* x *suntense* and *A. vitifolium* in lilac shades are also splendid. There is also a white form – *A. vitifolium* 'Album'.

If you put abutilons outside during the summer, don't forget that they are extremely attractive to winged visitors. The plant tends to form seed in large round pale green capsules but, unfortunately, they do not always flower. The best solution is to remove most of the capsules, unless you are hoping to do some plant breeding, and sow the seeds in the normal way. Sewing the seeds you have obtained poses no problem.

Abutilons must be brought indoors if the night temperature falls as low as 0 degrees celsius (32 degrees fahrenheit).

For summer arrangements I have chosen sunflower yellow. On the right you can see one of my favourite compositions. At one side, a tub full of lilies intensifies the overall effect with their green-yellow colouring. The yellow of this lily, 'Connecticut King', is repeated in the subtle tone of *Kirengeshoma palmata*, the pale yellow of pansies (*Viola* x *wittrockiana* 'Moonlight'), and the greenish-yellow of *Hosta fortunei* 'Aurea' in an old moss-covered pot. Making a contrast is the almost colourless beauty of *Carlina acaulis* var. *caulescens* in a very attractive honeycombed pot from Italy. Also from Italy is the small rectangular pot with a rounded lip housing the pink-grey *Echeveria* 'Rose von Nürnberg'. The same rosy contrast is found in *Cryptanthus roseus,* in the small pot on the left, which produces tufts of flowers on top of its wavy rosettes. In the tiny pot on the right is a *Nananthus villettii.*

On the left-hand page are the delicate flowers of *Hebenstreitia dentata* 'Attraction' (bottom left), an annual whose perfume only appears at night. Its flowers in the form of plumes act like torches through which the perfume passes into the night air. In the front of the picture are the last flowers of the perfumed *Petunia* hybrid 'Summer Sun'. In the pot (bottom right) the first of the gold blooms of *Trollius stenopetala*.

In the illustration on the far left is an arrangement in which *Tagetes* plays a major role. Overflowing the horizontally striped pot is just one *Tagetes signata* (syn. *T. tenuifolia*) 'Lemon Gem', a plant which grows exuberantly. It can also be found in other colours – 'Paprika', for instance, with its brown-red petals bordered with orange, and 'Starfire' which comes in all tones from lemon to brick red.

The photographs on these two pages can only give an idea of the many atmospheres that it is possible to achieve in a garden. Not just at the beginning of the season when everything is in flower, but also at the end of the summer, when the many different shaped seed pods (which, happily, nobody cuts off in this garden!) create a beautiful world of fading tints.

The composition of the colours of the overcrowded flowerbed of pots is very subtle, alternating with tones of pale yellow and blue. The elegant *Agapanthus* with its tall slim stems; the perfumed trumpets of the green-flowered tobacco plant (*Nicotiana* x *sanderae* 'Lime Green' – unlike other tobacco plants it has no scent); the cascades of *Lobelia erinus* 'Blue Cascade' and

Brachycome iberidifolia 'Blue Splendour'; and the vivid blue of *Cynoglossum amabile* 'Blue Shower' all play their large role. Here, too, *Eucomis bicolor* and *Cleome spinosa* also have a place.

It would be possible to complete the yellows and blues in these pot compositons with *Muscari*, varieties of *Scilla* and *Iris reticulata* among the blues; and for early yellows, with the winter *Eranthis* (aconite), small species of daffodils and early yellow *Primulas*. The soft tones of *Calendula* 'Cream Beauty' and 'Lemon Beauty' also add to the yellows and blues of the flowerbed, and are easy to sow. Placed in a small moist container, *Primula florindae* flowers in summer and its soft yellow corollas are always gracious. The trailing *Ajuga reptans* quickly covers pots with a curtain of green leaves and little blue spikes. The perfumed *Asperula orientalis* is an adorable blue annual which decorates many containers. Love-in-a-mist (*Nigella*) stays looking good long after flowering because of its handsome seed pods. Finally a pot of hyssop (*Hyssopus officinalis*) attracts the attention of small white butterflies.

BLUE ON BLUE

A roof garden makes an ideal background for a rich symphony of blue, in which the blue of the bouquets and plants is heightened by the varied blue tones of Portuguese pottery.

Left: the *Browallia* in its oblong porcelain trough on the right of the arrangement is crowned on the left by delphiniums. Together they serve as a background for a charming bouquet composed of the flat tops of the half hardy *Trachelium caeruleum*, the soft blue of *Scabiosa caucasica* 'Clive Greaves' and the intense blue of *Gentiana axilariflora*.

Below left, on the table, is a flowering display consisting of *Tolmiea menziesii* surrounded by *Hydrangea macrophylla* in various shades.

The flower arrangement on the right-hand page has many subtle variations. In the large jug hydrangea flowers are flanked by rich blue spikes of delphiunium – all sorts of tones are possible with *Delphinium* x *cultorum* 'Moody Blues', and elegant panicles of *Veronica longifolia* 'Blauriesin'. In the small porcelain container is the pretty delicate blue of the forget-me-not, *Myosotis alpestris* 'Blue Express', while the small jug repeats the delphinium theme.

The photograph above was taken in early June and shows an *Alygogyne huegelli* (formerly *Hibiscus huegelli*) with large lilac flowers which has already become quite bushy. By the time it is ready to come indoors in November, it will have flowered again. The colour of its flowers is repeated in the much smaller annual *Brachycome iberidifolia,* which you can see in the half-glazed pot on the left. On the right-hand side, the bright blue pots contain lavender and a small carnation with very blue leaves called *Dianthus* 'Blue Hills' which produces deep pink-purple flowers. One cannot but admire the enchanting marguerites. The ones illustrated here are *Osteospermum ecklonis* with shining white flowers and centres of acid blue grown from a cutting, and the Cape marigold *Dimorphotheca pluvialis* 'Glistening White' with white flowers and brown centres. Anyone who has grown some *Arctotis grandis* (syn. *A. venusta*) will note its resemblance to this plant. Whatever their type, they are always graceful in pots, flowering almost all the summer if you pick off dead blooms. In the front of the picture is a very young agave named *Agave victoria-reginae laxor* or *A. ferdinandi-regis!*

This large arrangement of delicate blue tints and lilacs is set out to great effect in three old zinc containers.

At the back of the picture is a large pot filled with *Agastache foeniculum* with its long flower spikes and aniseed scent which attract insects to the garden. In the middle the tendrils and flowers of a lilac-mauve passion flower – *Passiflora* x *alatocaerulea:* this plant is not hardy and must be taken in for the winter. The passion flower *P. synfordtii,* on the other hand, looks very much like it, but its roots can take temperatures going down to as low as -10 degrees celsius (14 degrees fahrenheit). In the container on the right of the picture is the late flowering *Liriope muscari* 'Variegatus' with fringed blooms, and, on the left, the beautiful blossoms of *Oxalis arifolia* (see also page 58). Placed on the round container in the front of the picture are some passion fruits with wrinkled skins – they have nothing to do with the species shown in the arrangement but seem to complement the composition.

The trailing violet *Viola hederacea* (top right) which, like the *Alygogyne* on the left-hand page, gives great pleasure to its owner, flowers throughout the summer but cannot stand a cold winter. It is therefore sensible to take it indoors to assure its protection (see also pages 84-85).

An early vision of spring is a little *Aquilegia flabellata* 'Caspar Innes' in an old clay pot (above). This plant maintains all the grace and beauty of its elegant flowering for a long time.

PLAYING

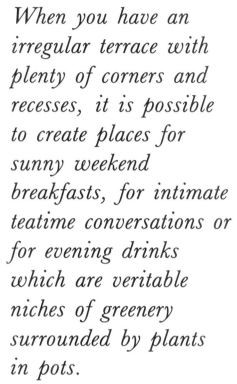

When you have an irregular terrace with plenty of corners and recesses, it is possible to create places for sunny weekend breakfasts, for intimate teatime conversations or for evening drinks which are veritable niches of greenery surrounded by plants in pots.

In the middle of the romantic terrace on the right a table and three benches, arranged in a semi-circle, are hidden behind a *Brugmansia* surrounded by plants. The way into this rustic dining corner is flanked by two lemon trees trained on bamboo frames. Of all the *Citrus* species, these are the ones that are most easily trained and are, therefore, very suitable to flank an entrance. On both sides of the passage pots are ranged in battalions. On the right, in front of a pot filled with *Hymenocallis* x *festalis* not yet in flower, is *Echeveria glauca* with its rosy pink flower spikes and *Aeonium arboreum* which has these mahogany tones from early summer.

What is so agreeable about this simple yet sophisticated setting is that you can, as I have indicated in the introduction, shift your plants around, relegating the less attractive ones or those which have already flowered to the back, and giving the place of honour to those that are in bloom. You can also put the accent on different annual plants each year. Here this has

WITH BORDERS

been done with pots full of the sky-blue marguerite *Felicia amelloides*.

The potted primula

A number of species of *Primula* grow astonishingly well when put in pots. At the top of the left-hand page is a charming example of a young *Primula capitata* var. *crispata* showing its first flower in a tightly packed head on a white dusted stem. On page 151 you can see that *P. auricula* is also very much

at ease when grown in a pot. The same goes for those species which need a great deal of water like the pretty *P. florindae* which produces its pale yellow flowers in summer – you can also find a version in a brick-red colour called 'Red Selection Drake'. It is necessary, of course, to keep these plants damp, not necessarily in a water-proof container but certainly in a pot placed on a saucer in which you should always keep a little water.

An array of pots

A show of pots devoted to just one species can be very spectacular because of the pattern it makes. Hydrangeas, which appreciate shade, are ideal for arranging in a line across a corner. At the bottom of the left-hand page, *Hydrangea macrophylla* has been chosen – the type that bears blooms in pretty tones of pale pink.

ALL SORTS OF PINKS

The word pink implies so many tints and tones, so many degrees and shades, that they are more than this chapter can cover.

Pink, which can be pale or bright, salmon or peach, is a colour for all seasons. One can have a 'vie en rose' even in the grey of autumn!

From all the colours that can be found in *Aquilegia vulgaris*

'Biedermeier' I have chosen examples in pale pink, deep pink and purple for the prettily coloured spring picture below. The fruits of this aquilegia are not as spectacular as those of *A. flabellata,* but last longer. The *Thalictrum aquilegifolium* 'Thunderbird', whose flowers form powder puffs, also keeps its charm for a long time, for after the rose-lilac flowers come tufted seed heads of a beautiful green, and then trembling winged seed pods in brown-purple

tints. Still with the spring picture on page 110, after its silvery lilies have flowered, *Allium karataviense* also has attractive round fruiting umbels which are ideal for drying and using in flower displays. In the front of the arrangement to the left, is a very beautiful *Geranium renaldii* which, with its rounded velvety blue-green leaves, still looks lovely after the pale lilac veined flowers have gone. A *Heliotropium arborescens* (syn. *H. peruvianum*) cultivated in the form of a bush adds a final touch to the whole ensemble. My experience with perfumed plants is that it is better to propagate them from cuttings rather than by seed, for the latter only rarely seem to retain their perfume.

From spring to frost

The *Lewisia cotyledon* (see page 111) flowers from spring until the first frosts. Out in the garden in a rockery these plants are hardy, but in a pot they tend to be more fragile and it is preferable to keep them indoors in a cool place during the weeks of hard frosts.

A spectacular spring

On the roof terrace of his house, Kees Hageman, who took most of the photographs in this book, has created some spectacular spring colours: sophisticated combinations of mauve, vivid lilac and spring yellow. On the far left a standard trained Indian azalea – *Azalea indica* (now called *Rhododendron indicum*) repeats the colours of the geraniums in the background (*Pelargonium* x *domesticum*) and those of the flowering fuchsia against the wall. At the beginning of spring a touch of yellow-green is added by *Euphorbia polychroma*. On this page the same tones reappear, although in a slightly paler form, with the ivy-leaved geranium *Pelargonium peltatum,* and a broom, *Cytisus* x *praecox* on the left-hand side of the picture, which has already replaced its scented flowers with green pods. The tall *Achillea millefolium* 'Moonshine', with its pale yellow flowers, makes a strong contrast to the pink flowers.

The pale rose of summer

Pale colours are not confined to spring. As shown in the picture below, summer also has its pastel tones. The place of honour is reserved for an *Anisodontea capensis* (previously known as *Malvastrum*) which I have grown as a standard and which is becoming more and more tree like. Its small flowers on elegant branches bloom for many months, and it is a species that is very easy to grow from cuttings. In front of it in a pretty basket-like pot are the blue leaves of *Sedum* 'Ruby Glow' which has a purple tone about it at the beginning of the year. And to prove that scented *Pelargoniums* don't always produce tiny flowers, the example here gives a splash of bright colour to the arrangement. At the extreme left are the flowers of a *Datura metel*.

To achieve still more summer pastel tints you can grow little pots of ivy-leaved toadflax, *Cymbalaria muralis,* which often lightly spills its little cushions over the rim. For perfume all you need do is to add some little carnations (*Dianthus*) in pale tones. For night perfume you might prefer annual stocks (*Matthiola bicornis*) which by day seem grey and insignficant, but which release an unsurpassed scent when evening comes. There are several hybrids of *Hemerocallis,* ranging from the palest pink to burgundy and purple, which grow particularly well in pots. You might, finally, choose a simple lily, preferably a scented one like 'Journey's End'. *Polemonium carneum* is one of the most charming varieties, with panicles of subtle pink. And if you are able to find one, you would appreciate the soft shell-pink bells of *Platycodon grandiflorum* 'Perlmutterschale'. *Prunella* x *webbiana* 'Loveliness' is a pretty little pale pink flower which also grows well in pots. *Crinum powellii,* another good choice, needs to be planted in a deep pot which will take its large bulb. The annual *Datura ceratocaula* is worth sowing in a large container for its beautiful perfumed flowers. *Amaryllis belladonna* flowers late in the season with rose-lilac bells, and the same goes for *Nerine bowdenii* 'Rosea'. Neither of these two bulbs is hardy and it is better, therefore, to plant them in pots.

On the left, the principle role is played by an example of the annual large-flowered *Lavatera trimestris* which is seen here both in its white form ('Mont Blanc') and its soft pink form ('Silver Cup').

Miniature delights

The art of raising miniatures, for instance of Bonsai, is well established in the botanic world. What is true for trees is also true for plants. But one cannot really enjoy these exceptional little blooms unless you can see them at close hand. So, while they are flowering put them on a table on which you can enjoy their pretty blossoms day after day.

In the group at the bottom of the page on the right are the elegant rose-purple flowers of *Allium farreri,* and in a melon-shaped pot a *Geranium farreri,* a miniature species of geranium. In the tiered pot is *Ptilotrichum spinosum* 'Roseum' with its pale pink flowers, while the small pot at the left contains *Pelargonium* 'Lilian Pottinger' with its beautiful scented leaves.

On the extreme right (small illustration, top) a superb specimen of *Cyclamen neapolitanum* shows off its flowers in the autumn. The corms of this cyclamen, like other late-flowering species, grow well in a pot and can also be naturalised easily.

An amusing story attaches to the rosette-shaped succulent with remarkable pink flowers (right). This plant was discovered in 1972 in the mountains of Mexico near Chihuahua. Its existence was kept secret for some time when it was given the appropriate name of

Tacitus. This was bracketed with the name *bellus,* even though nobody, at that time, knew that this little plant was, in fact, pretty. It is regrettable that it was eventually decided to replace the appropriate name of *Tacitus bellus* with *Graptopetalum bellum.*

I have planted in one of my oldest pots (bottom right) a charming mini-specimen with bright green leaves and flowers in the form of purple bells which give way to charming russet capsules. Nobody would believe that this is a simple rhododendron, but this miniature shrub with hairy stems and deciduous leaves is called *Rhododendron camtschaticum.*

On the opposite page the attractive trough decorated with the head of a lion was made in Italy; I have filled it with a *Hosta.* At the front of the container and to its left is a standard cultivar of one of the many Japanese maples (*Acer palmatum*), which grows very happily in a large pot,

A world of giants

It is obvious that this splendid *Bougainvillea* is not planted in a pot but in the earth in a hot country. This spectacular picture, can, nevertheless, act as a source of inspiration for fantastic colour combinations for a balcony, terrace or patio.

On the next page a group of superb neoclassical urns give the impression that they are really old because of a particularly successful finish. They were made in Greece but are photographed in Belgium, where they make ideal containers for dried flower arrangements.

On page 121 an attractive pale pot decorated with lions' heads contains a bunch of the extraordinary stonecrop *Sedum spectabile* placed in the centre of a growing patch of the same plant. Like many other plants of the same species, *S. spectabile* is perfectly happy grown in a pot (see, among others, that on page 63).

By pouring cement into a mould it is possible to reproduce any number of ornaments. Newly moulded pieces are not particularly aesthetic, but as soon as they begin to be covered in moss they acquire a charm of their own. As the same mould can be used many times, concrete garden ornaments are less expensive than

CONTAINERS

original carved examples. And by placing them in a humid shady spot, or bathing them with a weak solution of manure, you encourage the growth of moss.

The little frog on the right of the left-hand page has lived for several years between my barrel filled with scented leaved *Acorus calamus* and a large pot of beautiful blue-green *Sedum bithyricum* 'Glaucum'.

At the top of the left-hand page two containers and a swan that I have had for some time have already taken on a completely different appearance since I bought them. At the back of the picture is a quick-flowering Japanese lily (*Lilium speciosum* 'Uchida Kanoka'). In the same spot I have also sown some annual stocks, *Matthiola bicornis,* for the perfume that they give out on spring evenings, although, unfortunately their flowers are a drab grey. Behind the swan the elegant leaves of the silk tree (*Albizia julibrissin*) unfold majestically from a large pot decorated with Tudor roses. It has to be brought indoors to avoid heavy frosts. Heather fills the hexagonal container, while the swan is filled with creeping bugle (*Ajuga reptans* 'Burgundy Glow').

The leaf under which the tortoise is taking refuge is that of a *Gunnera manicata* (facing page, left). From its rounded nose to its curled up tail the tortoise measures 70cm (27½ ins.) long which gives some indication of the size of the gunnera.

I feel that these concrete figures should only be used in moderation. It is never a good idea to place several of them on one terrace, for inevitably a frog is hidden in a corner or the cat on the lookout is covered by vegetation.

On this page, a very old urn decorated with garlands and a stalking cat have found a place among silvery foliage and orange flowers. In the moss-covered urn are the notched silver leaves and orange flowers of a *Glaucium corniculatum* – not quite so well known, perhaps, as its sister with yellow flowers, the horned poppy *G. flavum* which self seeds so easily. All around are silvery tufts of *Cotyledon undulatum* 'Silver Crown'.

The bright green foliage and dark orange flowers on the right belong to *Gloxinia latifolia* (syn. *Seemannia latifolia*) which is flowering only six months after sowing. At the back of the picture are the large clear green leaves and the regal flower of *Haemanthus katherinae* which surprises me each year with its large powder-puffs of soft orange.

Chilstone

The ornamental objects and urns shown on these and the following two pages are all moulded, but they certainly cannot be considered ugly concrete objects. The owner of this garden has laid it out very elegantly with ornamental Chilstone items. In front of the *trompe-l'oeil* trellis (below) is one of the best pieces in the collection, 'Pope's Urn, recreated from a design by William Kent in 1744 for the gardens of the celebrated writer and poet Alexander Pope. The vase on the left is a copy of a fluted Roman urn (it comes with a lid which is not shown in this photograph). The column on which it stands comes in several different heights.

Garden ornaments by Chilstone are made from a mix of gravel and Portland cement. On the right-hand page you can see how good these ornaments look after several years. The weather and moss have given the decorative basket-patterned urns a most attractive look.

The lattice trellis at the back, which can be used to decorate or cover many kinds of walls, is composed of panels 160 or 180cm (63 or 71ins.) high and 50 or 90cm (19½ or 35½ins.) wide. The panels can also be used on their own, as can be seen in the picture. The little white garden which surrounds this charming pavilion has a lawn made of a scented carpet of creeping camomile, *Anthemis nobilis* 'Treneague', which never needs mowing.

Haddonstone

These elegant urns and ornamental objects were made at East Haddon in Britain. Such pieces are generally found in the gardens of many English country houses, even at Buckingham Palace and Windsor!

The basket-patterned trough at the extreme left is placed alongside a handsome Italian designed jardinière decorated with flowers inside lozenges. The large pot with a lattice pattern is copied from an Elizabethan design, while a Regency-style urn stands on a plinth, beside it two dogs originating from Italy. In this group of Haddonstone containers the decorative plants consist of several species of ornamental cabbage and taller plants in greeny-white, among which are ivy (*Hedera helix*), the leaves of *Euphorbia marginata* splashed with white, and a *Trachelium caeruleum* 'White Surprise' with white inflorescences.

Carved or moulded?

The difference between objects carved in stone and those made from a mixture of cement is obvious. On this page the beautiful example of a basket of fruit carved in stone comes from Italy and is made to order from old designs. On the left, a pair of moulded baskets. The chisel used by the hand of man obviously gives a much finer piece of work than does cement poured into a mould. But the price is very different too! On the left-hand page the background is provided by columns covered with climbers. These are two versions of the Virginia creeper, *Parthenocissus tricuspidata,* with three-lobed leaves, and *P. quinquefolia* which has five-lobed leaves.

ILVER FOLIAGE

There is no more sophisticated partnership than terracotta with silver foliage, though the latter harmonises equally well with green and mossy wood.

On the left a rather sombre arrangement of startling silver-blue *Agave utahensis* and *Kalanchoe tomentosa,* its downy silver leaves marked with chestnut brown. A dense flat silver carpet of *Raoulia subsericea* covers the pot at the front of the picture.

Just behind the *Raoulia* is *Tacitus bellus,* whose flowers are still in bud (see also page 117). A the back a slipper orchid, *Paphiopedilum callosum,* carries its delicately tinted flowers above leaves touched with silver.

On the right is a more simple arrangement. An antique wooden cheese mould banded with metal is filled with vigorous shoots of *Artemisia pontica,* beside it the handsome scented St. Bruno lily (*Paradisea liliastrum*). At the front, the tiny leaves of *Pelargonium odoratissimum* give off a penetrating perfume, while the white of the lily is picked up by the little camomile-like flowers of *Anacyclus depressus* with its silvery foliage. The fern on the right in the shallow pot is *Polystichum lonchitis.* A weather-beaten white marble bath in the background comes from the collection at Mentmore, and the initials of Mayer Amschel de Rothschild can just be made out on it.

A sea of silver at the end of summer

There are so many elegant silver-leaved plants to choose from that it is difficult to decide which ones to grow. However, the *Artemisia* family is, of course, always well represented in this silver sea. At the back of the picture below a large container is filled with the astonishing almost white *Artemisia stelleriana* which gives the impression of being a mountain of silver.

The stems of *A. arborescens* 'Faith Raven' are almost woody, but the general impression of the plant is lacy and fine. Another splendour is *A. schmidtiana* with its gossamer-like leaves (to the left of the picture).

At the front is marjoram (*Origanum majorana*). This is a superb herb, and if you bring it indoors in its pot during the winter you can keep it going until the next year. On the extreme left the large serrated silver-white leaves of *Centaurea gymnocarpa* are just visible and contrast well with the more delicate lace-like foliage of the artemisias. The tiny flowers of *Aster ericoides* 'Esther', and the pretty petals of *Tricyrtis stolonifera* add a few touches of late summer pink to the picture.

In the picture on the far left, a place of honour has been given to a delicate pale silver-blue beauty with pink bracts and tiny golden flowers. This is *Monarda punctata*, a plant which is not appreciated as much as it should be when hidden in the middle of a collection of silver foliage.

ILD WEEDS

So-called weeds can make wonderful flower arrangements, as the illustration on the right proves. And, as you can see on the left, field flowers also offer innumerable possibilities.

The point of departure for the arrangement on the right is a beautiful pot in the shape of an artichoke, and your garden may provide leaves that go well with it (in this case not, in fact, the leaves of the artichoke (*Cynara scolymus*), but the leaves of cardoons – *Cynara cardunculus* – which look very like it). Also in the pot is a member of the cow parsley family, *Heraculeum spondylium,* and the large black-berried umbrels of black elder (*Sambucus nigra*).

Pots for blanching

A word about Mediterranean cardoons. Everyone knows that their leaves are better if they are blanched by being covered in the spring. There are tall terracotta blanching pots especially made for this purpose with a hole in the top and a lid. When the right moment arrives you put these bell-shaped pots over the cardoons (as well as seakale – the blanched leaves and stems of *Crambe maritima* are absolutely delicious to eat) and cover them with a large pile of manure. In that way in the darkness and with the heat generated the leaves grow very fast and very white. The lid allows you to look inside the pot from time to time to see whether the leaves are ready to be harvested.

On the page on the left I have assembled several wild plants in glazed pots from Spain, one of which is overflowing with rusty-red sorrel flowers and branches of small yellow 'mirabella' plums, the fruits of *Prunus cerasifera*. On the ground to the right is a pot of *Artemisia vulgaris*. On the left of the table is an elegant little pot of *Galtonia princeps* and another of *Hemerocallis* 'Green Flutter'.

135

SEEDS, PODS AND BERRIES

This arrangement of plants and seeds that I picked haphazardly while on a walk has all the charm of spontaneity. Equally, these plants can easily be grown from seed in your garden.

1. *Lupinus cruckshanksii.* An elegant species of lupin with blue-pink clusters and velvety pods.

2. *Atriplex hortensis* 'Gold Plume'. One of the many fine species of spinach, this plant not only produces pretty flower spikes but also delicious leaves for salads.

3. *Papaver somniferum* 'Minipod'. Capsules of the small opium poppy adapt themselves wonderfully to flower arrangements.

4. *Nicandra physaloides* 'Black Pod' (the apple of Peru, or shoo-fly plant) produces these attractive purple-black lanterns after its pretty clear blue flowers. They make an unusual addition to dried flower arrangements.

5. *Lepidium latifolium.* A member of the cress family (*L. sativum*), this produces seed pods on long stems which are ideal for dried flower ar-rangements, though it grows rather too enthusiastically in the garden.

6. *Bulbine annua.* An annual lily that will perfectly happily reseed itself and which produces attractive capsules after its yellow flowers.

7. Two tobacco plants, *Nicotiana rustica* with its green flowers, and *N. tabacum* with pink flowers, both eventually produce these large clusters of attractive plump capsules.

8. *Nigella sativa.* A pretty little sister to love-in-the-mist, this aromatic nigella with its cream flowers and long follicles dries very well.

9. *Gilia thurberi, G. capitata* and *G. leptantha,* all have blue tubular flowers which eventually produce amusing round capsules which are much sought-after for dried flower arrangements.

10. *Omphalodes linifolia.* The dainty white capsules follow ravishingly pretty flowers which look like white forget-me-nots.

11. *Datura stramonium.* Its fruits, like prickly apples, are splendid for flower arrangements but they must not be touched by children because the plant is poisonous.

12. *Iberis amara* 'Mount Hood' and 'White Pinnacle' both make bunches of pretty white flowers followed by attractive seed pods in the form of serrated discs. 'White Pinnacle' is scented.

13. *Nigella ciliaris* (syn. *orientalis*) produces crowns of follicles.

14. *Lepidium campestre.* Delicate and sophisticated, it dries well but, like *L. latifolium* (5), tends to take over in the garden.

15. *Reseda odorata* 'Machet'. The sweet-scented mignonette also produces splendid seed heads which eventually change to rust tones.

16. *Reseda alba,* the white mignonette. A little less perfumed than *odorata,* it produces elegant flowers and open-topped capsules.

17. A piece of cork in the pot helps absorb the moist heavy sap which comes from the stems of newly picked flowers.

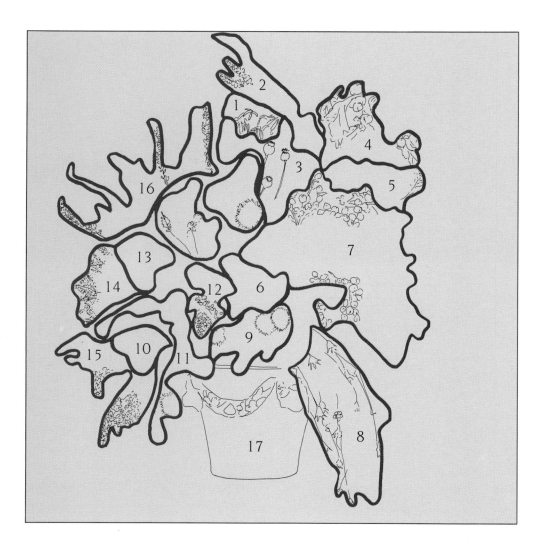

# A GREEN BOUQUET

Although I have no particular prediliction for green plants myself, many flower arranging enthusiasts go into raptures over them.

Here are seven which are about to open: a splendid day indeed in the plant world!

1. *Cerinthe major* (syn. *glabra*) has masses of soft blue-green leaves. The plants grow very tall and in great profusion. Its flowers, a wonderful addition to an all-green arrangement, are bunches of slender bells which are yellow-green with purple-brown centres. Swarms of bees are attracted to these plants and buzz around them in summer.

2. *Amaranthus* 'Green Spire' has slim spikes of bright green flowers.

3. *Ipomopsis elegans* (syn. *Gilia rubra*). If the summer is hot, this plant produces elegant green furry stems before flowering. The flowers themselves are a vivid red.

4. *Cerinthe minor.* A smaller version of *C. major* (1), its stems fan out into flowers made even greener by their bracts.

5. *Ammi visnaga.* The much larger *A. majus* is often used as a cut flower, but I have used the smaller *A. visnaga* in this arrangement. At the back you can see its deeply-cut leaves and in front its fantastic flower umbrels.

6. *Elsholtzia ciliata.* A plant that is not well known, this has pretty green-beige blooms which will stay flowering for weeks if watered.

7. *Bupleurum rotundifolium.* Much appreciated for flower arrangements. If the winter is particularly mild it is almost hardy.

8. These bulbous pots decorated with fine garlands are available in many different sizes and colours (in plain terracotta or with a brown finish). A thin area in the base means you can pierce it for a drainage hole, though if you intend to use such a container as a cache-pot or vase you obviously don't make a drainage hole. This pottery is very dense and, therefore, less porous than most terracotta, so it is possible to use it without putting a saucer underneath.

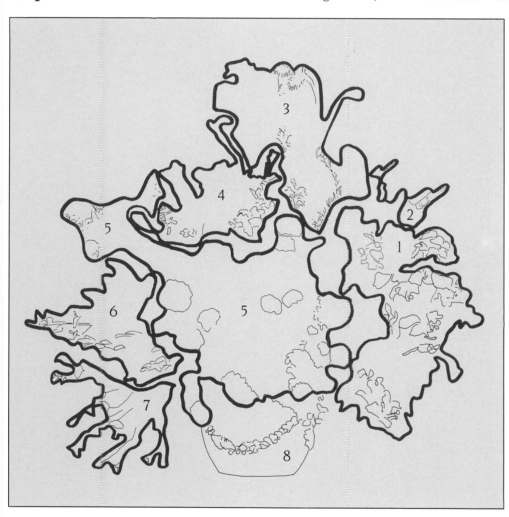

EAVES AND THEIR LINES

Leaf shape is very important when growing plants in pots. If all your plants have narrow leaves, for instance, your composition will have all the allure of a field. On the other hand, if you limit yourself to varieties with large leaves you end up with a heavy looking arrangement lacking in interest.

On the left-hand page, under the pale green canopy of an indoor lime tree (*Sparmannia africana*) which has grown to an impressive size, is the brilliant dark green of a gardenia, the rosette shape of a robust *Agave filifera* and the slender tall stems and white flowers of *Acidanthera bicolor*. This composition is a good example of what can be achieved with contrasting forms of leaves. The pots and terracotta fruits are French.

The leaf forms shown on this page also provide a wide range of contrasts. At the front of the picture, the leaves of *Hosta sieboldiana* 'Glauca' present a compact shape while, under the large foliage of a *Brugmansia,* are the reed-like leaves and salmon-pink flowers of a *Hemerocallis* which gives a touch of elegance to the picture. Towering over the hedge at the back of the picture on the right, is a large nut tree which has been pruned to give a dense effect.

On the far left, an elegant hand-made pot contains a large-leaved plantain (*Plantago major* 'Rosularis'), a plant much in fashion in the 16th century and coming into favour again.

To the left of the charming basket collection (centre left), in the middle of their glossy dark green leaves, are the prolific fruits of *Skimmia japonica* 'Nymans'. They are particularly splendid at this green stage of their development, and the plant contrasts well with the woolly pale green leaves of germander (*Teucrium crispum* 'Marginatum') and the blue-green cushions of *Saxifraga aizoon* var. *baldensis*. At the front is a basket of handsome squashes.

Near left, *Melianthus major,* a plant which, when fully grown, produces bunches of mahogany flowers to accompany its pretty serrated blue-green leaves.

Far left, in a large shallow container, are the lemon-yellow flowers of a poppy (*Papaver myiabeanum*) which is already flowering in its first year. Beside this is *Origanum rotundifolium,* a plant which produces pretty shrimp-pink flowers. At the front of the picture is an exuberant little *Cymbalaria muralis* 'Alba'.

Left, the elegantly shaped leaves of *Solanum laciniatum* are offset by bunches of brilliant green berries. These eventually turn a deep yellow-orange, when they are much appreciated by birds.

143

BASKETRY

Basketwork harmonises very naturally with plants and fruits as the examples on these two pages show.

The problem with growing plants in baskets is that the latter tend to deteriorate quickly due to their continual contact with wet soil, though florists' baskets are generally sold with internal protection in the form of a plastic lining. Baskets are perfect for arrangements of flowers that are not too sappy, but less suitable for growing plants in. If you do grow plants in a basket, you need to make drainage holes in the plastic lining, though this will eventually mean the bottom of the basket deteriorates. The best solution is to use baskets as cache-pots, lining them with something protective – the most practical lining is a plastic pot which is normally not very beautiful but often the perfect shape to fit into a basket.

On the right is a random collection of baskets and plants, while on the left is a more formal arrangement of old and new baskets at the Chateau de s'Gravenwezel. The twisted basket on the right, on an 18th century Italian console table, was woven from the stems of a wisteria.

CAST-IRON

In the 19th century cast-iron was much used for garden urns, and for tables, chairs and benches for outdoor use. As a general rule cast-iron urns last a long time, especially if they have drainage holes in them, when there is little risk of frost damage. This explains why these highly decorated objects are still relatively easy to find.

The urns photograped here come from several different collections but you should be able to find similar items without much difficulty.

On the left, a Victorian table harmonises perfectly with a cast-iron drinking fountain on the wall. The plant with silver leaves which trails over the table edge is the everlasting *Helichrysum petiolatum*.

The shape of cast-iron pots can be very important if they are to follow a particular pattern, for instance lined up in front of a range of windows in a courtyard (far left). But plain cast-iron containers painted the same colour can also make a very attractive array for a display of plants (left).

Cast-iron pots can be used as ordinary containers, bearing in mind that they are generally provided with drainage holes, but it is also necessary to provide a waterproof container inside. This could perhaps be a jam jar or a plastic bucket – anything, as long as you cannot see it. Another possibility is to line the urn with a solid sheet of plastic or plug the drainage hole with a cork and then fill the pot with flowers poked into moist moss.

Below left, the last picture in this chapter devoted to cast-iron and the first in the next which deals with purple-brown plants. In these black painted cast-iron urns I have grown *Astilbe simpiicifolia* 'Sprite' in the tallest urn, together with the trailing violet, *Viola labradorica*. Two containers are filled with *Heuchera americana* 'Palace Purple', a new variety which can easily be grown from seed. In the other containers are, on the left, the pale colours of *Corydalis cheilanthifolia* and, at the front of the picture, the exuberant beige of *Sedum dasyphyllum*. This needs a rich soil if it is put into anything as restraining as a cast-iron urn and should be given fertiliser regularly. This does not apply to the houseleek *Sempervivum tectoram* or to similar plants that live naturally on fissures in the wall or among roof tiles, as these are generally content to grow in soils that are low in nutrients.

BROWNS AND PURPLES

Plants with marvellous purple-brown and chocolate shades are shown on these four pages. As can be seen on the preceding page, the tones of such leaves always make for a rich effect, especially when associated with black urns.

Top right a *Primula auricula* is shown against an almost black background: forming what is almost a still life, an old clay pot is filled with young primulas to capture the first rays of spring sunshine against a background of black-painted wooden planks.

On the right is a more modern looking arrangement, this one of wild plants including *Amaranthus* and numerous forms of *Chenopodium quiona*. This is one of the most important edible plants found in the high mountains of Chile and Argentina and it is eaten in numerous ways; the leaves are treated like spinach. A large amount of seed is extracted from the flowers which, after treatment, is made into flour. Here a selection of purple and green colours is shown, but a similar arrangement is also possible with cream and beige. You could just as well order and sow seeds of one of the many *Amaranthus* or of *Chenopodium quiona* (whose cultivar names are 'Ishiga', 'Amachuma', 'Kaslala' and 'Pizankala').

On the left-hand page are several different chocolate-coloured plants or plants with a

chocolate perfume. In the top left-hand corner, a glimpse of early spring with a cast-iron urn full of houseleeks, another containing carnivorous plants, and a pot of *Euphorbia amygdaloides* 'Rubra', whose spring flowers form a pretty contrast with their brown-purple leaves. At the back of the picture the green spikes of *Acidanthera* which will soon begin to change to a mahogany colour.

Beside this picture, top right, is *Eugenia myrtifolia* with its brown tinged leaves clipped in the form of a sphere and perched like a mother hen above three smaller plants with chocolate-coloured leaves: one is *Pelargonium* 'Chocolate Soldier', with brown markings on its leaves, another *Pelargonium* 'Chocolate Tomentosum', with a scent of peppermint chocolate. The illustration below this shows *Eugenia myrtifolia* in flower, its little white pompons formed by the stamens. You can see clearly from the brown buds that this *Eugenia* is a close relation to the clove. These aromatic buds come from *Eugenia aromatica* (recently rechristened *Syzygium aromaticum*). After flowering the brown bud turns into a little red berry, which explains its common name Australian bush cherry. A number of other varieties of *Eugenia* with edible berries also exist, although they are not easy to find.

Below the detail of the flowering *Eugenia myrtifolia* on page 150 is the fragile *Cistus* x *cyprius*. This produces a purple-brown spot at the base of each petal. Still on page 150, bottom left, is a species which not only produces truly purple-brown flowers but also, when the sun shines, blooms that give off a real chocolate smell. This is *Cosmos atrosanguineus* which cannot be grown from seed; its white tubers must be dried off during the winter and stored away from frost.

The last illustration on page 150, bottom right, is the charming white-flowered geranium, properly called *Geranium sessiliflorum* ssp. *novaezeelandiae* 'Nigricans'. At the end of the summer its elegant pendulous leaves take on russet and orange tones.

A terrifying looking growth (right) shoots out from a chocolate-coloured succulent plant – *Jovibarba heuffelii* 'Chocoletta'. This was produced unexpectedly from seed produced by some varieties grown from cuttings. It is fascinating to obtain novelties like this in unexpected colours.

FRUITING PLANTS

Some examples of attractive fruiting plants make no demands on you other than to be planted in containers.

On the left are a couple of pots with seedlings of *Eucomis bicolor* and arum *Zantesdeschia albomaculata*. In both these cases I broke the fruits over the surface of the pot, and in spring covered them with a good layer of manure through which the miniscule seedlings pushed their heads. In this way it is possible to obtain pots full of small seedlings.

On the right is a *Calla palustris* which stays good looking for a long time as its its seed head turns to a mass of red berries.

Some beautiful fruits

Allium siculum (syn. *nectaroscordum*). This can be put in a pot in the shade where it will make large umbrels with hanging flowers striped beige-brown followed by lantern-shaped seed heads.

Anemone multifida. After green-white flowers, this produces seed heads that look like little white strawberries.

Anthyllis vulneraria. An old medicinal plant which produces egg-yolk-yellow flowers. Afterwards each seed comes wrapped in a covering of filmy 'paper'.

Aquilegia flabellata. This plant is mentioned on page 107.

Argemone grandiflora. Immaculate paper-thin white flowers are followed by bluish capsules.

Asclepias syriaca. The cotton wool flower is an ideal plant for a large tub. After one flowering, when its honey perfume attracts the bees, it produces slender capsules that look like green wigs.

Dioscorea balcanica. This form of the yam is a vigorous plant that needs staking; its unusual three-cornered fruits are fleshy and flecked chestnut-brown.

Dryas octopetala. This plant belongs, believe it or not, to the rose family, and is a charming evergreen sub-shrub with white eight-petalled flowers and graceful fluffy seed heads.

All varieties of *Helleborus* produce splendid crowns of green capsules after flowering.

All varieties of *Hosta* produce attractive solid looking club-shaped capsules after their white or pale lilac flowers.

Iberis, Reseda, Omphalodes and other seeding plants which you can grow in a pot can be seen in the arrangement on pages 136 and 137.

Isatis tinctoria, the woad plant, is a biennial which, after its yellowish flowers, makes long branches of pendulous green pods.

Lunaria annua 'Sissinghurst White', commonly known as honesty, produces silver paper 'coins' after pretty white flowers.

Muscari armeniacum. After producing little blue flowerheads, this plant carries spears of shiny black seeds.

All varieties of *Nigella* produce very attractive fruits.

Pulsatilla vulgaris and *P. vulgaris* 'Alba' are just some of the pretty flowers that bloom in the spring, their large lilac or white flowers resembling anemones. Afterwards they form feathery seed heads.

Scabiosa prolifera and *S. stellata* 'Drumstick' are two annual scabious. The first has pale yellow flowers, then fruits in the forms of rounded umbrellas, the second has pale or aquatic blue flowers followed by almost turquoise spherical seed heads on stems which make them suitable for all sorts of arrangements.

THE ART OF THE PAST

On the following pages we show some examples of old containers. They range from robust pots for everyday use to gracious 17th century marble urns, and come in many different shapes.

On the right, a zinc table with its mottled reflections and a collection of 19th century pots with soft patina make for delicacy and simplicity. Four of the containers (on the floor to the left) were designed for everyday use and once housed food – probably cereals. A fine oil jar on the table has a hole for a tap, and to its right is an upturned dish, and three elegant pitchers. On the floor on the extreme right is a huge ridged wine jar.

The dish and the oil jar on the table and the food jars on the floor come from Calanda, a village in Spain, where the pottery is not turned but pressed and sculpted from layers of clay laid one on another and then finished by hand.

Two totally different containers which date from the beginning of the 19th century. The one on the near right was made by Royal Doulton in England for storing provisions. The other, far right, an urn ornamented with serpents, was made in France.

If you want to cultivate plants in a container that has never had a drainage hole in it (basins and oil jars don't usually pose this problem) it is necessary to make several holes from the outside with great care. If the idea of doing this in a fine old piece of pottery doesn't appeal to you, then lay pieces of of broken pots or tiles in the bottom to help drainage, or use water-retaining granules in the compost, but, above all, never place pots without drainage holes out of doors where they could collect rainwater.

Plant stands, on which it is possible to store a large number of pots during the winter, were once seen in every orangery. They are now much valued as decorative objects as the pictures on these pages show. The one on the left is made of wrought-iron, the one below of wood and cast-iron.

The first shows a large collection of scented-leaved geraniums (*Pelargoniums*) lined up for winter, plants which normally appreciate plenty of light. I have this collection together so that each time I handle the pots and gently touch the leaves they release their many different perfumes – mint, peppermint, rose, lemon, orange, peach, pepper, nut, nutmeg and even cedar.

Some plants have large velvety leaves – *Pelargonium tomentosum,* for example, while others have long stalks and small leaves, like

P. odoratissimum. Some push their way up to the light with little crinkled leaves – *P. crispum* 'Variegated' for instance, while others have a more elegant trailing habit – *P.* 'Lilian Pottinger'. Apart from being a species with scented leaves, there are also plants which have perfumed flowers. *P. cortusifolium* produces white flowers with red markings which release a soft but perceptible rose scent during the day. *P. gibbosum* has a rather strange appearance with its scalloped blue-green leaves; its soft yellow flowers release a fragrant perfume in the evening. And then there is a *P. triste* which has a rather drab colouring but gives off a wonderful scent which can only be described as that of nutmeg and which attracts moths in the evening.

The new orangery at the Chateau de 's Gravenwezel gives shelter to several beautiful examples of contemporary plant decoration. The flow of its arched windows, seen here on the left, gives marvellous emphasis and background for floral decorations. Below, two superb 18th century urns glazed in browns and yellows.

On the left a white Meissen chandelier overhangs winter arrangements housed in, among other containers, late 18th century lead urns.

On the table at the front of the picture, to the right of a Queen Anne chair, is a very old terracotta pot and a charming wooden bowl.

The floor of this orangery is ex-tremely simple being composed of old brick paving laid on a bed of sand. When plants are housed in a conservatory or orangery in this way it is useful to have this type of flooring because it rapidly absorbs surplus moisture, while the legs of the furniture are not directly exposed to the damp.

To look after plants which live permanently in a conservatory, like climbers that drape themselves lazily over columns, it is best to make large holes in the paving and plant them as deep as possible in good soil. Sand by itself is not suitable for growing plants, and even in soil beds in a conservatory it is wise to put down some fertiliser about twice a year.

The splendid 18th century water tank on the far right is dated 1729. Typically English, a second example, also in lead and in the garden of an antique dealer and decorator, is photographed in *The English Garden Room* by Elizabeth Dickson. The rainwater collected in these containers is, of course, ideal for using on certain plants, above all species that cannot stand chalk, varieties of *Camellia* for instance.

On this page terracotta containers, flanked by tortoises guarding the little wooden bridge, are filled with rushes which rustle in the wind.

A fountain or rainwater tank make perfect features in the pot garden. You can either water your plants with the rainwater, or grow plants directly in the tank. The very pretty 17th century carved stone fountain (left), where water is pumped out of the mouths of two lions, is in one of the outbuildings of the Chateau de 's Gravenwezel.

The pink stone baptisimal bowl, below, dates from the end of the 17th or beginning of the 18th century. It is usually best to use a container like this as a cache-pot; it is also better for the plant, for it allows for the circulation of air and regulates the water supply.

A simple urn or water trough can be the basis for a very decorative effect if it is in a niche or recess (see following pages). In the first picture an old stone urn is placed on a carved stone plinth, both of them dating from the 18th century. The Italian marble bust dates from the 17th century. On page 169 a late 19th century water trough is surmounted by a recently added mask out of which water drips.

In the absence of a niche or hidden corner, a tank cut in the open air can also make an attractive feature. But you must never forget to empty it when frosts are expected.

This lovely 18th century dolphin fountain flanked by large leaves of bird of paradise plants (*Strelitzia*) comes from Portugal. At the front of the picture is a simple display of clay pots filled with a variety of *Clivia nobilis*.

A 17th century Florentine urn (right), with beautiful veins threading through the marble, remind one of 'Calacatta vagli rosato' which can still be found at Lucca.

The urn, large basin and pillar (left) are in white Carrara marble. The decorative urn is one of a pair made in Italy in the 18th century for an English client.

VEGETABLES

Against the wall of a shed in my garden I have made a terrace of vegetables. An aubergine with small round white fruits grows out of an onion pot and a bushy cucumber is placed in a strawberry pot. There, too, are rhubarb stalks gleaming as if covered in varnish, American blueberries, which offer the birds a splendid feast, and the gourd 'Patty Pan' with its round fruits.

On the left hand page, a table is covered with exotic plants that have been grown under cover or in cloches. Throughout the summer the pot with two pepper plants looks extremely good, the baby peppers developing one after the other into beautiful deep yellow fruits. This is a variety called *Capsicum annuum* 'Golden Calwonder' which must always be sown in a warm place in the spring so that it is well advanced by the time summer comes. In front is a pot containing the first two tendrils of *Sechium edule*. Under the cloche in the front of the picture is a papaya fruit (*Carica papaya*) which I did not grow myself but simply bought. Under the tall cloche which tops an old pot with handles, are two courgette plants, 'Sweet Mamma', which I mention on page 178.

Below is a close up of the interesting gourd 'Patty Pan' which spills out of its pot. The fruits are very pleasant when they are ripe, but if you cook them when they are young, they have an exceptionally delicate flavour.

Lollo Rosso and Sweet Mamma

'Lollo Rosso' is the name of a type of salad leaf with crinkled red edges which is not only extremely decorative but also much appreciated by gastronomes. As for 'Sweet Mamma', this is a form of deep green courgette which can be seen on the right.

It only took half a packet of seed of 'Lollo Rosso' to fill all the containers on the right-hand page. These lettuces produce such pretty curly heads (see also page 186) that I haven't the heart to cut them. It is an even more attractive plant when it bolts (see the small photograph right). I am also considering making arrangements with some of the curly leaves, though at the moment this is no more than an idea.

Strangely enough my two 'Sweet Mamma' courgettes (which you can also see under the cloche on page 174), seem to grow better in the confined space of the old pot with handles (which I always feed with plenty of compost) than the five other plants in the large pot (far right). Nevertheless, it is interesting that you can grow courgettes successfully in containers.

All the reds

Apart from 'Lollo Rosso' with its decorative frills, there are a number of other lettuces which come in the same colours.

Among the cabbage lettuces is 'Inka' or 'Wonder of Four Seasons'. Among cos lettuce there is a red species called 'J.W.22'. There is a leaf lettuce 'Red Salad Bowl', and an iceberg called 'Rosa', to say nothing of the incomparable oak-leaved lettuce with its indented leaves.

There is a small Italian salad leaf of a deep red called 'Rossa di Verona', though it doesn't actually belong to the lettuce family (*Lactuca sativa*) but to the chicory family (*Cichoria intybus*).

If you want to have a red vegetable terrace, you could try growing red spring onions which go under the name of 'Santa Claus', and there is a species of endive called 'Robin' bordered in purple-red which can be cultivated without earthing up. For the winter you can even have red Brussels sprouts which are called 'Rubine'.

Beta vulgaris, sold under the name 'Ruby Chard', is very seductive in its red livery, while *B. vulgaris* 'MacGregor's Favourite' with its deep colouring, which was grown in England as far back as the 19th century, is not just for eating but for decorative use as well.

FRUIT

The culture of edible plants of any kind can easily become an obsession. Just as collectors of Citrus *exist (and the genre consists of a good two dozen species – see pages 50-55), there are enthusiasts who fill their greenhouses or conservatories with fruiting climbers (see pages 22-29), and others who cultivate any small area with edible plants in pots (see pages 176 and 177).*

For years now, among the ornamental plants on my terrace, I have had a host of edible plants and herbs – bay trees, for example (see pages 40-41), or an olive (*Olea europaea*) which, despite having flowered, has up to now never given me any fruit. Then there is, of course, my collection of *Citrus* which perfume the air deliciously and give me succulent fruits, to say nothing of the elegant blueberry, *Vaccinium corymbosum,* already full grown, which stays outside all year

AND HERBS

and which has wood almost as red as that of the dogwood (*Cornus alba*) in winter. Its curtain of white flower clusters during the spring are transformed a little later into beautiful deep blue berries of which the birds are very fond. This bush is illustrated on the extreme left of the picture on pages 176-77.

For a long time, too, I have tried to raise a pomegranate (*Punica granatum*) to the point where its thin branches will give me beautiful big red fruits, but for the moment I have had to content myself with its vivid red flowers with their crumpled appearance.

Even though it does not produce fruit out of doors, a bush or standard *Feijoa sellowiana* or *Acca sellowiana* looks very decorative. Its edible fruit is called pineapple guava. You can see a flowering branch illustrated on the right.

The velvety curved petals, rose-pink outside, grey-lilac inside, have long vivid red stamens.

I was very surprised when, having bought two *Sechium edule* and left them a little too long in their plastic bag, to see that they had germinated and produced fine white roots, as you can see at the front of the photo below left. I then planted them, and the photograph at the top of the page on the left

shows the result. The 'chayotte', as it is called on the Continent, comes from the cucumber family (*Curcurbitaceae*) but, unlike the other numerous varieties of this family, it is a plant that climbs on its own tendrils. Planted in a warm sheltered place it will develop plenty of shoots and fruits each year.

In the arrangement on the left you can see basil, red orach (*Atriplex hortensis* 'Cupreata'), and the aromatic herb which is called 'shisho' in Japanese cuisine, *Perilla nankinensis* 'Atropurpurea Laciniata'; you can use the leaves, flowers and seeds of this herb, which can easily be cultivated in a pot and can reach the height of a man. See it in flower on page 184.

The long terracotta trough on the far left contains green basil, *Ocimum basilicum;* below it is the purple variety 'Dark Opal'.

181

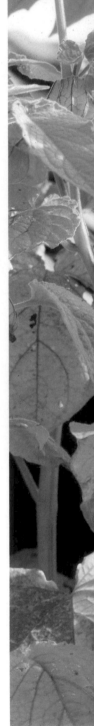

From grapes to wild strawberries

The tortuous trunk of the vine and the elegant form of the little fig tree (*Ficus carica*) make a decorative pattern against the black sides of this barn. They both need to be brought inside to shelter if there is a severe winter.

It is amusing to transform a vine into a weeping standard tree You can also do the same thing with wisteria. First take one straight shoot and train it upwards, tying it to a cane. Then pinch out lateral shoots as they appear, letting bunches of grapes develop on the top growth only. Equally interesting results can be obtained with almost any climber trained it this way.

Three illustrations of plants with edible fruits are shown on this page. On the left, a *Physalis peruviana,* otherwise known as the Chinese gooseberry which, in the space of one season is covered in soft, fresh-tasting berries. These plants are less hardy grown in a pot than if you put them out in the open ground, but there are some advantages with the former method: planting of the seed can be done earlier and, if cold weather comes unexpectedly, the pots can be brought inside giving the fruits a chance to ripen.

On the right (top) is a close-up of the strange flower of *Solanum melongena.* I cultivate this plant in an enormous pot. The roots find plenty of nourishment in the large amount of soil, and I get an abundant supply of pale yellow egg-like aubergines. It is, of course, important that fruits and vegetables cultivated in pots are given plenty of fertiliser.

The little white fraise de bois, *Fragaria vesca* 'Yellow Wonder' (right), hides it fruits and in doing so cheats the birds who are less likely to see it. Its fruits (shown also on page 186) ripen in their pots in the same year the seed is sown.

The tree tomato, otherwise known as the La Paz tomato, goes particularly well with this group. Scientifically known as *Cyphomandrea betacea,* it comes, like the common tomato, from the *Solanaceae* family. Grown in a pot it produces a charming perennial bush with oval fruits which are usually yellow, striped with green, turning red as they mature. The tree tomato cannot stand a cold winter and must therefore be brought in to avoid frost.

Swathes of sweet potatoes

The sweet potato *Ipomoea batatas*, looks very much like our ordinary potato (far left). Having said that, it does not come from the potato family, *Solanaceae*, at all but from that of *Convolvulaceae*. You can see the difference when the climbing stems are ready to flower and the astonishing little dark red blooms appear. If you want the benefit of a good harvest, then it is best to plant them in a deep pot where their little tubers will develop well. But if you want to obtain a really large yield you should plant sweet potatoes in a conservatory or cold frame, when they take from 140 to 150 days of sunshine to ripen.

Garlands of apple cucumber

The apple cucumber, whose botanic name is *Cucumis sativa* 'Maliforme', has made a recent appearance on the market.

Early one year I pricked out some little plants in a large strawberry pot (left). The result exceeded all my expectations. The garlands of trailing stems tumbled over the container, enveloping it in a curtain of fresh green foliage followed by small yellow flowers, after which the little beige hairy 'apples' appeared. Apple cucumbers are cultivated in the same way as gherkins.

If you have a warm place in which to grow things you could try *Momordica charentia* (the balsam pear) or even *M. balsamina* (the balsam apple). All the climbers cited here are from the cucumber family, *Curcubitaceae*, which prefer a tropical or subtropical environment.

TRAWBERRY POTS

Originally designed to take strawberry plants in small quantities, the strawberry pot allows the fruits to develop high and dry, warmed by the sun. But it can also take a mass of other plants in its little pockets.

The three strawberry pots, left, make a simple but effective picture. The one on the far left contains the creamy white berries of strawberry *Fragaria vesca* 'Yellow Wonder' (see also page 183). In the centre is the salad lettuce 'Lollo Rosso' with its frilled leaves (see also pages 178-179), and on the right the violet 'Milky Way'.

Why not herbs?

Strawberry pots make particularly good herb gardens – many varieties of thyme, especially, go well in these containers. Choose the herb you like and plant a different type in each pocket.

Other herbs to try are, for example, savory, *Satureja repens* (see also page 195), and the vigorous mint, *Mentha pulegium*. Basil also looks good grown in a strawberry pot.

In a larger container you could put a complete mix of herbs – each pocket containing a different plant. It would be a shame not to include the scented creeping mint, *Mentha requienii* – for although it is not really edible, its perfume is exquisite.

Most creeping plants will hang in a curtain over the rims of their containers. Think for a moment of the tinted rose-lilac flowers of *Ajuga reptans* 'Burgundy Glow', or the many other types of this plant in different colours. Or you might prefer the beige flower spikes of *Acaena* or a spring pot, perhaps, filled with *Anemone pulsatilla* (syn. *vulgaris*) with seed pods as soft as silk. Planted in a strawberry pot and put in the most obscure corner *Galium ordoratum* (syn. *Asperula odorata*) will, nevertheless, scent the air heavily. The same goes for *Oxalis acetosella* 'Rosea'. Little violets like *Viola odorata* and the creeping *V. labradorica* (see page 149) only need a little light and a little care. *Stachys olympica*, (syn. *lanata*) covers a pot with its silvery wool while *Alchemilla alpina* – a smaller form of the common *A. vulgaris* – makes a silver cloak with a white lace underside.

Strawberry pots will also house many species of succulents like *Sedum, Sempervivella, Echeveria* and *Orostachys* (see pages 56-67). Planted this way, succulents can pass the summer out of doors and the winter inside.

In the spring it is possible to fill strawberry pots with bulbs like hyacinth, *Crocus, Scilla, Muscari* or snowdrop (*Galanthus*). These can then be transferred into open ground after flowering to make way for summer blooming plants. You can also sow annuals like *Lobelia, Hebenstreitia* and the biennial forget-me-not (*Myosotis*), or summer flowering bulbs like *Eucomis autumnalis, Sprekelia* and *Babiana,* in strawberry pots.

MARROWS, PUMPKINS AND SQUASHES

There are many impressive members of the cucumber family whose fruits come in a multitude of forms and in colours ranging from the most vivid orange to pale celadon green. Such plants only need a season to cover the ground, a compost heap or a peeling wall with vigorous fresh green leaves and a profusion of yellow flowers. And then there are the fruits... delicious in soups, they are also natural decoration. That is why on these and the following two pages the main part is played by the marrow and members of its family.

On the garden table opposite a pot of 'Sweet Mamma' courgettes (see pages 178-179) rampages over a collection which includes a pumpkin from Surinam on the left and, on the right, some squashes, *Citrullus vulgaris* – like the marrow from the *Cucurbitaceae* family – which can be preserved and used for decoration. Here too are 'New Dragon' and 'Blue Hill' powdered with grey.

Marrows are not only grown in pots. If you want to have a large harvest then it is better to sow them in open ground. But the fruits harvested can be used to fill pots, the many different tones contrasting well with the various colours of terracotta.

Butterflies don't only feed on the nectar of flowers, they are also very fond of the sugary taste of overripe fruit (below).

Harvest festival

For a dozen years or more now more and more of the marrow family have been cultivated for their subtle colours. It is true, for instance that the enormous yellow pumpkin 'Centenaar' is only grown for its size (in popular giant pumpkin competitions), that 'Sweet Mamma' gives pure green fruits, while 'Gold Nugget' produces pretty yellow fruits, and so on. But if you sow them near to each other you have a good chance of obtaining some interesting crosses the following year. Harvest the ripe seeds yourself, wash them, dry them and put them in a cool airy spot until the time comes to sow them. If you want to obtain seeds of a particular variety like 'Butternut Squash', for instance, you can always buy a ripe example from a greengrocer and use its seeds. The same thing can be done with exotic species like the pumpkin from Surinam on the preceding page. It is best to sow seeds in a greenhouse or conservatory (as you would melons) otherwise they will not ripen.

A year's harvest is displayed on these two pages, all coming from a small piece of ground. It's far too much, needless to say, for the personal use of one family, so friends and neighbours benefit too.

191

LONG LIVE HERBS AND SPICES!

A blade of lemon grass or vetiver, a little grated ginger – there is nothing like home-cultivated herbs and spices to give your dishes an exotic flavour.

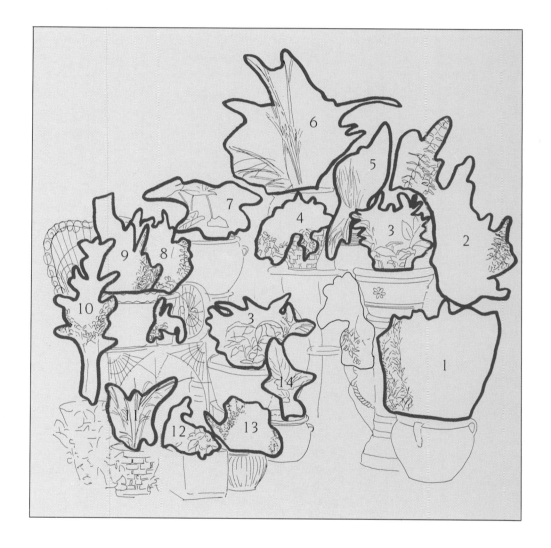

1 *Rosmarinus officinalis*. Rosemary. Despite several severe winters I still grow it outdoors in a pot.

2 *Aloysia triphylla* (syn. *Lippia citriodora*). This lemon verbena is freshest of all lemon-scented plants.

3 *Zingiber officinale*. Ginger, a single leaf of which gives off a strong scent. The oval pot contains the rhizomes which produce the shoots. Freshly-grated ginger is far more pleasant than the powdered form sold in shops.

4 *Mentha rotundifolia* 'Variegata'. Round-leaved mint is delicious as a herbal tea, beautiful in a bouquet.

5 *Allium tuberosum*. The chive not only has a delicate flavour but pretty flowers throughout the summer.

6 *Cymbopogon citratus*. Fresh blades of lemon grass are much more satisfactory than the dried form.

7 *Xanthosoma sagittifolium*. Taro. A member of the *Araceae* family, this has the reputation of being the best tropical green vegetable. The leaf is cooked like spinach.

8 *Mentha suaveolens*. This plant has a tinge of ginger about it; its leaves are striped with yellow.

9 *Helichrysum angustifolium* and *H. serotinum*. The curry plants whose silvery leaves in the form of perfumed needles give off a strong aroma which is unforgettable when served with chicken or eggs.

10 *Glycyrrhiza glabra*. This is the botanic name of liquorice whose rhizomes not only have a sweet taste but are also used in medicine.

11 *Cymbopogon nardus*, or citronella, is not used for cooking but its oil discourages mosquitoes.

12 *Ocimum basilicum* – the best aromatic plant in the world, basil.

13 *Thymus citriodorus* 'Silver Queen'. A silvery thyme with a lemon perfume.

14 *Curcuma domestica*. Turmeric, the Indian saffron, comes from the ginger family *Zingiberaceae*. Its yellow rhizome is peeled and used in curry.

Gold in the kitchen

Pictured below is a collection of golden plants that are particularly popular in any kitchen. In the urn with handles on the left is a beautiful display of gold-splashed thyme with a lemon scent (*Thymus* 'Doone Valley'), while in the urn on the right is a clump of variegated gold origano (*Origanum vulgare* 'Aureum'). The pot at the front has some thyme in it too, but it is dominated by young variegated sage plants (*Salvia officinalis* 'Aurea').

In the lower centre picture is scented savory, *Satureja repens*, with its white flowers.

Shades of purple

The collection of containers below display tints of purple and pink. *Mentha pulegium* grows rapidly, even when confined to a pot. An exuberant flowering origano (*Origanum vulgare*) is not just a delicious herb for cooking purposes but is also a plant that attracts butterflies. The cabbage white, for instance, often flies over the little pink flowers.

On the left, peppermint, *Mentha* x *piperita* var. *citrata* with its familiar scent, plunges its roots deep into the soil. The flower of this mint is particularly good with fruit salads, desserts and drinks.

In the pot with a decorated border is purple sage (*Salvia officinalis* 'Purpurea').

Finally, the strawberry pot, top centre picture, has been turned into a thyme garden: ordinary thyme, *Thymus vulgaris* in the centre with *T.* 'Doone Valley' in its little pockets.

195

Herbs and spices are appreciated for their elegance and simplicity everywhere – from cottage to chateau garden.

It's pleasant to put pots of them on tables and along passageways so that you can run your hand over the leaves and release their aroma as you pass.

Above, two small stone 19th century plinths are pedestals to healthy pots of thyme. On the left the table in *pietra serena*, a very fine-grained stone, dates from the 18th century, but it is relatively easy to obtain modern copies of antiques like this.

REPOTTING PLANTS SUCCESSFULLY

As a general rule plants are sold in plastic pots which, despite their ugliness, are the choice of horti-culturists because they are straight sided. Their ungainly appearance can often be compounded by another fault: they are increasingly coming in shapes which are the same, or almost the same, diameter at both ends, turning them into perfect but inelegant cylinders.

As most containers tend to narrow towards the bottom, it is necessary, when buying a pot, to measure its diameter at the base, rather than the top. In general, therefore, you should buy a terracotta pot, for instance, that is larger than the plastic one it is replacing. That may cost more but it is not so bad for the plant, which probably needs more space when you buy it.

If you have a plant growing in a plastic pot, tap it several times against the ground, and squeeze the sides gently to make sure that the tangle of roots is not stuck to them. If the plants have been in a plastic pot for a long time, it is sometimes difficult to extricate them. In that case you should take a large knife and cut the plastic from top to bottom, taking care

not to harm the root ball. Hold the knife parallel to the pot side and slide it straight down to the bottom. The rootball can then be eased out without any difficulty.

If you want to repot a plant which is growing in a terracotta pot, first of all water it copiously, let it drain, then gently tap the top edge of the pot against a hard surface, tip the pot upside down and ease the plant and earth out.

One often comes across rounded containers that curve in at the top. These may be good to look at but should be confined to housing permanent plants or for cultivating annuals. Otherwise, if your plant outgrows the confines of the curved pot, it is impossible to extricate it without damaging it. If it is a perennial, however, then it is relatively easy to divide it and take it out in two or three segments without doing harm.

One could also cultivate bulbs in rounded pots as the bulbs don't have to be taken out in one clump when they are planted out, but can be eased out separately.

Some gardeners cut the roots of a plant if they have to remove plants or shrubs that have become too large for their containers, cutting the top growth in the same proportion. You can do the same sort of thing in the case of a rounded container: make a vertical cut with a knife through the root ball and pull out a piece of the plant. Repot the plant and cut back some of the top growth to match.

If the rounded pot is an important one, and you don't want to remove the plant, you can always take out the top soil, ease away as much soil as possible from round the roots with your fingers and replace it with fresh soil, preferably mixed with a little compost.

Fertilisers

When you think about fertilisers, never forget that pot plants are

much more deprived than those growing in open ground. It is therefore absolutely essential to give them a supplementary feed at least twice a year. I cover my pots with a thick layer of well-rotted manure, especially in the spring when plants which have passed the winter indoors come out into the fresh air.

I repeat this during the summer (before the end of July), and also fertilise *Citrus* plants, but with great care because too much will result in a plethora of shoots and fewer flowers and fruits.

Knowing that many plant owners dislike the smell of manure, I have tested two sorts of soil-based compost which you can buy. Neither of these smells (one is compost that has passed through earthworms) but you must mix the fine coloured powder in with the soil to ensure that the unpleasant yellow colour doesn't spread around the terrace.

If you have bought plants whose soil contains little white granules for better aeration you will find that they constantly tend to come to the surface. I generally cover them by putting a layer of earth on top of the compost.

Watering

Always take care that pots are not filled right up to the top with soil as this makes watering difficult. You should be able to cover the surface of the soil with 2cm (1in.) of water.

Saucers are indispensable during very hot dry periods, but harmful if there is prolonged rain. If rain has set in, it is better to remove the saucers or to empty them every day. The root balls of plants will rot rapidly if they are left soaking in water, exceptions being water-loving plants like *Primula florindae*, arums, *Gunnera manicata* and water mint (*Mentha aquatica*).

In dry weather it is absolutely vital to water plants every day, though if they have a large saucer you can perhaps miss a day or two. To make sure that air rich in oxygen penetrates the soil, it is best to put a small amount of water in the saucer and a lot on the surface of the soil so that it is all covered. You will hear gurgling sounds which show that the water, as it percolates through, is followed by fresh air.

To each its own

The plants we cultivate on our balconies and terraces come from many different countries and therefore need very different soils. It is important, therefore, to find out the most appropriate compost for each one.

Commercially-made compost is used for many plants because it consists of a mix of peat, clay and sand enriched with fertiliser and an acceptable amount of chalk. Sometimes granules are added to help aerate.

Here are the mixes suitable for various plants:

Fuchsia and Agapanthus

Fuchsia and *Agapanthus* are quite happy in ordinary compost and it is only necessary to add fertiliser twice a year.

Citrus species

Orange and lemon trees and similar species like a little gravel added to a mix of garden soil, compost and sand. You can also find a specially mixed compost on sale for plants of this kind.

Chrysanthemums

Chrysanthemum frutescens. These plants with pretty daisy-like flowers enjoy a heavy soil, preferably 60 per cent clay mixed with 30 per cent compost and 10 per cent sand.

Lantana

Lantana, like *Fuchsia,* is satisfied with shop-bought compost but it is a good idea to add 10 per cent sand.

Brugmansia or Datura

To get ravishing trumpet-shaped blooms each year, plant these in a mix of one part clay, one part compost and one part peat.

Plumbago

This plant likes the same soil mix as *Citrus.*

Nerium Oleander

The oleander, which is easy to propagate by cuttings but balks at opening its buds, likes a mixture of part garden soil, part peat.

Agave

For the *Agave* and similar plants, use a mixture of 70 per cent clay to 30 per cent sand. These plants love a heavy soil made permeable by the sand.

For good drainage be sure to cover the holes in the bottom of pots with pieces of clay tile or something similar to make sure they don't become blocked. On top of this put a layer of drainage material to a depth of about 5cms (2ins.). This could be a layer of gravel, in which case it is best to cover it with a layer of synthetic fabric which ensures that the compost does not drain down through the gravel.

# THE WINTER JOURNEY

Though certain pots can spend the winter out of doors without risk, others must be brought in because the material of which they are made cannot withstand the cold. However, the difficulty is to tell precisely from the look of them which ones can resist rain and frost, for some apparently strong pots will break into a thousand fragments at the least drop in temperature.

The most prized pottery is not necessarily stronger than the pieces you have bought cheaply, and one manufacturer's product is not necessarily better than another's. There are, however, several definite rules to follow to ensure your containers spend winter in the best possible way.

The first rule is that any pot which is to winter outdoors must have a drainage hole, combined with a good layer of stone chips, gravel or something to help with drainage. If not the water stays in the pot, and if there is frost it freezes, swells and cracks the pot.

If the pot is outdoors but under cover, and if it is the kind where you can empty the water out, frost poses less of a problem.

It is necessary, therefore, to bring in any pots or other containers without drainage holes before the temperature really falls, though most pots will cope with a little frost. Barrels in which aquatic plants are grown are an exception. It is very difficult to bring them indoors, so to avoid problems it is important to make a hole in the surface of the ice if the water freezes, and to be sure that it does not close up again. If you keep an eye on this hole, then you can be sure that the water is not frozen below the surface, and that the wood is not under pressure and will remain intact. If there are fish in the barrel, they need to be taken in before the onset of severe frosts, for if the water freezes then it is practically impossible for the fish to survive let alone feed. Put a layer of synthetic fabric over the surface to prevent the water from freezing.

To make sure that most of the water runs rapidly through pots with drainage holes in them, you could put them on a couple of blocks of wood or four stones. I particularly recommend this for flat terraces where water tends to remain on the surface. In this case the pot is forever taking up moisture, water doesn't escape from the soil, and if the pot becomes frozen at the bottom, damage will be done to the container.

In old country houses or chateaux where marble or stone statues, vases or urns decorate gardens in climates that are not always favourable for these materials, you will find that these objects are often wrapped in straw and then in a waterproof cover for the winter. The latter is important, because if you allow the marble or stone to absorb water, it freezes in frosty conditions and becomes damaged.

Obviously a terracotta pot is very porous and is more quickly damaged by frost than something

less absorbent. Glazed pots finished in a high temperature are generally less porous and resist the absorption of water. But they do not breathe as much and are, therefore, less suitable for plants.

Pots whose outsides are decorated with garlands, masks, braids, etc., are easily damaged by frost. After having seen how they are made I can understand why. Years ago I saw large pots being decorated with garlands in Italy. The manufacturer, who had many different decorative moulds, let me choose which ornaments I wanted. The decorations were made, moistened, then stuck on to a freshly turned pot with clay. Needless to say the edges are loosely stuck in place and if water penetrates the ornament it tends to come off. It would be safer to stick them on with tile cement. These ornaments are actually carved on more expensive pots which makes them less likely to be damaged as a result of frost.

The most sensible thing to do with vulnerable pots, or the most expensive ones and those that are decorated with ornaments susceptible to frost, is to use them for half hardy plants which you bring in during the winter These include all species of *Citrus,* as well as bay, different varieties of *Eugenia, Melianthus, Echeveria* and other subtropical succulents, as well as non-hardy bulbs (*Hymenocallis,* species of *Eucomis, Zantedeschia* and star of Bethlehem (*Ornithogalum arabicum*) to mention just a few). These bulbs need little care because they don't need light or fresh air – they can therefore spend the winter in a dark dry place, sheltered from frost and preferably placed on shelves. It is important, nevertheless, to check from time to time that none of the bulbs have started to grow; if they have, separate them from the others and begin to water and fertilise them.

Protecting the root ball

If you are more worried about frost damage to plant roots than to pots, you should choose hardy plants. Most of the hardy perennial species can stay outside in a pot during the most severe frosts without any problem. For instance: *Hosta,* practically all the lilies (with the exception, of course, of *Lilium longiflorum*), *Sedum spectabile* and *S.* 'Ruby Glow', *Aquilegia,* species of *Geum,* all the mints and other aromatic herbs.

One way to protect clipped box, which is not totally hardy, in pots is to line the inside of the pot with plastic or pieces of polystyrene. I am not particularly keen on this idea, since the root ball is not in contact with the 'breathing' side of the pot. In the case of severe and persistent frost it is better to muffle the pots in straw, a layer of reeds and then plastic. At a time like this it is a good idea to bring small pots of box indoors (though not large ones which are obviously not transportable), as well as *Ligustrum henryi* and *L. delavayanum.*

The large barrel filled with *Gunnera manicata* (page 81) has a special frost regime. At the first sign of frost I cover this splendid but not hardy plant with an old fabric cover. If the frost is hard I put a sheet of plastic over the barrel and its contents. And if a period of really severe frost is announced I cover the entire barrel with bales of straw. This solution may not be very handsome but it doesn't last for long and one can always use the straw under shrubs or strawberry plants. Those who have a conservatory or a frost-free greenhouse and who have enough strength to move their barrels should naturally bring them in for the winter.

PHOTOGRAPHIC LOCATIONS

May and Axel Vervoordt
Chateau de 's Gravenwezel
Sint Jobsteenweg 64
B-2232 's Gravenwezel
Province of Antwerp, Belgium

Pages 16, 18-19, 28-29, 30-31, 32-33, 50-51, 52-53, 55, 73, 98, 129, 144, 147 (top), 148, 158-159, 161, 162-163, 165, 166-167, 168, 172-173, 196-197

The antique shop is open Monday to Friday from 9-12.30 and 1.30-6. The chateau is closed during July and on Mondays in August.

Ineke Greve
Maison 'de Dohm'
De Dohm 48/50
6419 CX Heerlen
The Netherlands

Pages 8-9, 17, 21 (top), 48, 57, 124-125, 141, 146

Ineke Greve's garden is open to visitors each year on the third weekend in June and the fourth weekend in August. Garden ornaments may also be purchased.

Fernande Hora Siccama-des Tombe
Flowerservice
Boschweg 6
3651 LV Woedense Verlaat
The Netherlands

Pages 44-45, 91, 120-121, 126-127, 135, 145, 147 (bottom), 164

Flowerservice is open Monday to Saturday, preferably by appointment. Phone 01724-8850.

Walda Pairon
Giardini
Kapellensteenweg 544
B-2180 Kalmthout-Heide
Province of Antwerp, Belgium

Pages 10-11, 12-13, 14, 34-35, 63 (top), 97

Giardini is open Fridays and Saturdays from 10-6; other days by appointment only. Phone 666 74 17.

Anton Schlepers and Henk Gerritisen
Jardins Priona

Schuineslootweg 13
7777 RE Schuinesloot-Slagharen
The Netherlands

Pages 74-75, 76, 86 (below left), 92 (below left), 100 (below left), 102-103, 188

Priona gardens are open from 1 June to 30 September, Thursday to Saturday from 12-5, and on Sunday from 2-6.

Yvo and Yselle van Orshoven
Heymansweg 3
B-3694 Neerglabbeek
Province of Antwerp, Belgium

Pages 22-23, 24-25, 26-27, 72, 190-191

Elisabeth de Lestrieux

Pages 15, 40-41, 56, 58-59, 60-61, 62, 78-79, 80-81, 82-83, 84-85, 87, 89, 93, 94, 96, 99, 101, 106-107, 109, 110, 114, 116-117, 122-123, 130-131, 132-133, 134, 137, 138, 140, 142-143, 149 (below), 150-151, 152-153, 154-155, 156-157, 160, 174-175, 176-177, 178-179, 180-181, 182-183, 184-185, 186-187, 189, 192, 194-195

# ILLUSTRATION CREDITS

Kees Hageman
Pages 2, 8-9, 10-11, 12-13, 14, 16-17, 18-19, 20-21, 22-23, 24-25, 26-27, 28-29, 30-31, 32-33, 34-35, 36-37, 38-39, 40-41 (large illustration), 42-43, 44-45, 46-47, 48-49, 50-51, 52-53, 54 (below), 55, 56-57, 60-61 (below), 63 (top), 64-65, 66-67, 68-69, 70-71, 72-73, 74, 78, 80 (below), 84 (below), 85, 86 (centre), 88, 90-91, 95 (below), 97, 98, 104-105, 108, 111, 112-113, 115, 118-119, 120-121, 122, 124-125, 126-127, 128-129, 132, 134-135, 140-141, 142 (below), 143, 144-145, 146-147, 148-149 (top), 153, 156-157, 158-159, 160-161, 162-163, 164-165, 166-167, 168-169, 170-171, 172-173, 174-175, 176-177, 189, 190-191, 196-197

Rudolf Bom
Pages 6-7, 15, 40 (top left), 54 (top), 58-59, 61 (top), 77-79, 80 (top), 81, 82-83, 84 (top), 86 (top), 87, 89, 92 (top), 93, 94-95 (top two illustrations), 96, 99, 100 (top and centre), 101, 106-107, 109, 110, 114, 116-117, 123, 130-131, 133, 136-137, 138-139, 142 (top two illustrations), 149 (below), 150-151, 152, 154-155, 178-179, 180-181, 182-183, 184-185, 186-187, 192-193, 194-195

Anton Schlepers
Pages 75, 76, 86 (below), 92 (below), 100 (below left), 102-103, 188

INDEX